IGNITE YOUR INTUITION

CANADA OH CANADA!!

IGNITE YOUR INTUITION

Improve Your Memory, Make Better Decisions, Be More Creative and Achieve Your Full Potential

To MACKENZIE + BRETT, BEST OF THOUGHTS!

CRAIG KARGES

CK

Health Communications, Inc.
Deerfield Beach, Florida

www.bcibooks.com

**Library of Congress Cataloging-in-Publication Data
is available through the Library of Congress.**

Library of Congress Catalog Number: 99-62387

© 1999 Craig Karges
ISBN-13: 978-1-55874-676-3
ISBN-10: 1-55874-676-5

Publisher: Health Communications, Inc.
3201 S.W. 15th Street
Deerfield Beach, FL 33442-8190

Cover artwork by Paul/Jay Associates, Bellaire, Ohio
Cover design by Lisa Camp
Cover photography by Mark Campbell, Prestige Photography, Wheeling, West Virginia

To Charlotte,
my extraordinary wife,
the love of my life and soul mate,
because without her
nothing matters

Contents

Acknowledgments

To Ron Martin, Dr. Barrie Richardson, Myriam Ruthchild, Lon Osgood and Richard Webster for their inspiration.

To my personal manager, Clinton Ford Billups, Jr., for believing in me.

To my parents, William Joseph and Cecelia Byrel Karges, who did the best they could with what they had—me!

To Peter Vegso, Teri Peluso, Matthew Diener, Lisa Drucker, Kim Weiss and all the wonderful people at Health Communications for making my first book a reality.

Introduction

The most beautiful experience we can
have is the mysterious. It is the foundation
of all true art and science. Without it,
we would be as good as dead.

Albert Einstein

For more than twenty years, I have earned my living as a "mystery merchant." I entertain audiences through the creation of mystery. As an "extraordinist," I simulate, demonstrate and duplicate the unknown, the unexplained and the unbelievable, seemingly by the power of the mind. (See About the Author at the end of the book.)

I have been very fortunate. My performances have taken me halfway around the world, appearing on television, at universities, in theaters and for major corporations. I like my performances to go beyond entertainment.

I want them to challenge my audiences' minds. It seems to work. No matter where I appear, I notice a great curiosity among the people who experience my performance. They want to know what is "real" and, more importantly, how they can learn to do these types of things themselves and how they can apply them in their everyday lives. This is why I wrote this book.

You see, I believe ordinary people are capable of extraordinary results. We all possess near infinite capabilities far beyond what the senses can perceive and what the mind can understand. Far beyond our wildest imagination. My intention is to provide a context within the pages of this book so that you can begin experiencing greater things in your life than you ever thought possible.

There is no reason for you to live an ordinary life once you wake up to the fact that you have extraordinary capabilities. Nothing is beyond your ability; nothing is impossible. As you read the pages of this book, you will be awed by your own mind, and you will be given the key to unlock the power within. You will discover how to get what you want in ways that you've never experienced before.

Some of you may approach this material with a skeptical "show me how this can be so." That's all right . . . I'm like that sometimes. On the other hand, I believe the cynical "this just can't be" can separate you from your natural mental gifts.

My best results happen when I am open to greater possibilities. I encourage you to be open to higher and more powerful possibilities. Motivational expert Dr. Wayne Dyer says, "You'll see it when you believe it!" Start right now. Einstein said, "Imagination is everything, it is more important than knowledge; it is the preview of life's coming attractions."

I say give yourself permission. Open yourself to possibilities that enable you to achieve far greater things than you ever thought possible. Set your imagination free—let it soar! Join me now on an extraordinary journey into your own mind. We will have a lot of fun, and I think you will be amazed at how powerful you really are.

Have a good journey!

Craig Karges

1 | The Extraordinary Computer Between Your Ears

The growth of the human mind
is still high adventure, in many ways
the highest adventure on Earth.

Norman Cousins

Your brain weighs about three pounds and it looks like a soft, wrinkled walnut. Pretty unimpressive looking at first glance. However, it has been in the making for about five million years. Whether you consider what it does or how it is constructed it is, by far, the most extraordinary organ in your body!

The human brain can store more information than all the libraries in the world! It is the cause of that violent outburst that you were so embarrassed about as well as the force behind the best idea you ever had and the

1

most charitable action you ever took. Your brain regulates all bodily functions and is responsible for your most primitive behavior as well as your most sophisticated accomplishments. All of your thoughts and emotions, indeed your personality, is inside that three-pound organ. You can receive a heart or lung transplant and still be yourself but if you were able to receive a brain transplant, you would no longer be you! Scientists have studied the brain for hundreds of years yet it remains so mysterious that many consider it humankind's ultimate frontier.

Your brain is a biological organ but it is also like an amazing machine, a supercomputer. It is miraculous! Your brain is truly one of the most amazing things in the universe. Think of it this way—the human brain is the only object capable of contemplating itself!

We, as human beings, tend to sell ourselves short. We stand in awe of computers, yet inside each of our brains lies ten times the amount of AT&T's entire communication networking system! We marvel at other animals like dolphin or ants. We can sit and watch an ant colony and be fascinated by it. How do they create such a complex structure? How do they communicate? An ant has about five hundred brain cells. That's the amount a person loses from drinking one glass of wine! But don't worry, we each have about 100 billion brain cells—that's as many as there are stars in the sky.

Each brain cell, or neuron, connects with all the others. Imagine, 100 billion electrical connections going on inside your head right now! Think of it this way: Imagine everyone in the world (about 5.5 billion people) talking on the phone to each other at the same time. That's a complicated image, isn't it? But to get an idea of the complexity of what is happening inside your head, you have to expand on this image. Take those same 5.5 billion people, put them on eighteen telephones each, have them all talking to each other at the same time and, if you can picture that, you can begin to understand the complexity of the communication process inside your brain!

If each neuron could only touch two other neurons, the number of possible configurations in your brain would be two to the 100-billionth power! That number would take you about nine hundred years to write out at one second per digit! In reality, because each neuron connects with all the others, the possible configurations are impossible to understand.

These busy little neurons send, receive and store signals that add up to information. Everything we do and all we know depends on the transfer of signals from neuron to neuron. A neuron has one big tentacle, its axon, and many smaller ones, its dendrites. The axon sends the signals which are received by the dendrites of other neurons. This is an electrochemical process that occurs at a point between cells called a synapse. This is as technical as we are going to get (aren't you happy!). But let me give you an extraordinary fact about dendrites, the receiving tentacles of the neuron. Believe it or not, we have over 100,000 miles of dendrites in our brains! In other words, the total length of dendrites in your brain could encircle the Earth—four times!

You might think that as we develop as human beings, the amount of connections among the neurons in our brains would increase. However, it appears that the opposite is true. There may be more connections in an infant than in a fully developed adult. Development seems to be about refining certain connections and not about making new ones.

Think about this: In the first weeks of life, a baby's babbling includes almost every sound of every known language! However, infants lose their ability to make sounds that aren't in the language they are learning to speak. The point is that the brain has enormous potential to do many things, such as learn the thousands of languages in existence, but we may only learn one or a few. What human beings are capable of is astounding; what we accomplish is often disappointing.

Can your brain physically grow? Consider this extraordinary experiment conducted by Mark Rosenweig and Marion Diamond at the University of California at Berkeley. The scientists took three brother rats and separated them into one of three environments:

1. Enriched: One of the brothers was placed in a large cage with other rats. This group was given new toys to play with daily, as well as food, water, etc.

2. Standard: One brother was placed with two other rats in a small cage with food and water.

3. Impoverished: One brother rat lived by itself with food and water.

The experiment concluded that the rats in the enriched environment had an actual increase in the weight of their brain! Ten percent was average.

And, what about the idea that we only use 10 percent of our brain? This figure and similar ones have been thrown around for years. I have been guilty of doing it myself during my entertainment and speaking engagements. Some people argue that only 10 percent of the brain has been mapped. We know that huge sections of the brain can be damaged and we can still function normally and we know that damage to certain small areas of the brain can be disastrous. Perhaps all of our brain is used at some point. We don't really know. What we do know is that we are far from knowing the limits of the mind's capabilities and our full potential. Compare your brain to your computer. Most of us only use a small percentage of our computer's power; it is the same with our personal computer power, our mind power.

In many respects, the brain is like a supercomputer. Scientists have spent more than a decade trying to develop a computerized version of the brain called a neural network. But these neural networks are very primitive when compared to the human brain. For example, while the human brain contains 100 billion neurons, its electronic counterparts typically contain the equivalent of a few thousand neurons (called neurals), or less. Each neuron in the brain has at least forty-six different attributes, such as the ability to interpret what you see or what you hear. The average electronic neural has about five attributes. Robert Hecht-Nielson of HNC, Inc. (a neural network firm in San Diego) says creating a brain-like computer is hundreds of years away. He likens the creation of this theoretical computer to the difficulty of developing spaceships that fly faster than the speed of light.

The entire notion of creating computers with artificial intelligence (A.I.) has been steadily losing ground. In the

1970s and 1980s, scientists specializing in A.I. were confident that they would someday replicate human intelligence by creating a computer that could learn and reason. Marvin Minsky was one of those scientists, a pioneer in A.I. In 1970 Minsky felt that within three to eight years a computer with the intelligence of an average human would be a reality. Thirty years later, no one has even come close to creating a machine that thinks like a human.

What about the chess-master-defeating IBM supercomputer, Deep Blue? As you probably recall, Deep Blue defeated grand-master Garry Kasparov, and this fact hurt some human egos. But let's put this in perspective. Deep Blue is still just a machine. Do we really think any less of humans because we can't run as fast as a car? Because we can't fly like an airplane? Because we can't add as fast as a calculator? Perhaps some human egos were bruised by the defeat of Kasparov because while many people can accept being surpassed by machines in mechanical tasks, they believe chess to be a creative as well as a mathematical endeavor.

Deep Blue is a two-million dollar, 1.4-ton supercomputer with thirty-two microprocessors and 512 support chips that was not designed to reason or learn, but rather to do one thing—crunch numbers. By doing that, it could come up with strong chess moves because the human brains of Deep Blue's programmers successfully reduced chess to a mathematical game.

Let's take a look at how you can use more of your extraordinary brain! What would you say if I told you that when you finished reading this chapter (and applying what you've read), you will learn to think like a genius? Accelerated learning experts have developed techniques based on the idea that you can become more creative and productive by using your whole brain.

What do I mean by this? Our brain has two hemispheres, the right and the left. They share our thinking and the control of our body. The left half of the brain controls the right side of the body and the right half of the brain controls the left side. Each hemisphere seems to specialize in certain functions.

The left brain's specialities are spoken and written language, logic, number skills and scientific concepts. Work that might primarily involve the left brain are bookkeeping, laboratory jobs and the like.

The right brain excels in recognizing patterns and shapes and how they relate to one another. It also seems to contribute most to insight and imagination. It is the hemisphere that appreciates art and understands humor. The work of a musician or architect draws heavily on the right hemisphere.

We need to strive to balance these two hemispheres. Creativity consultants say that left-brain dominants can learn to use their right brains by forcing themselves to daydream, draw and become more open and aware of their surroundings. If you feel you are a right-brain dominant, you can tap into your left brain by forcing yourself to take notes, ask detailed questions, make concrete plans and organize things through the creation of systems. At first, you may be uncomfortable when consciously shifting to using more of either hemisphere. But after a while, it will be second nature, and your brain will be balanced!

Here's another technique to master more of your brain power when it comes to reading information. In this day and age of information overload, we are often swamped with things we need to read and process. One of the best methods for retaining information is to range read. This is how it works: You first get an overview of the book by reading the table of contents and chapter headings, before you actually begin reading the book. By doing this, you implant the book's main ideas in your mind, paying special attention to those that interest you the most. This way you don't spend excess time reading the sections that don't pertain to you. While I would love for you to read this entire book cover to cover, feel free to practice range reading with it as it covers a wide variety of topics.

Jump start your brain by practicing brainstorming. Write down your problem or goal and then just quickly think of solutions. Write them down as quickly as they come to mind. The key is not to censor yourself. Write down the wildest, most absurd ideas. When you're finished, play with your ideas, placing them into categories or putting diverse concepts together. The results can surprise you.

When brainstorming, one of the most productive techniques is called mind mapping. It's a process of taking notes that mirrors the brain's thinking process. Instead of taking linear notes (outlining, for example) which are controlled by the left brain, mind mapping uses colored pens which stimulate the right brain. Draw a central picture in the middle of the page. Shooting out from the picture are smaller images and single words with connecting lines drawn from one idea to the next. The principle is that free association encourages new ideas and unlimited thinking, while traditional note-taking stifles people.

Any time you're taxing your brain, you should take hourly brain breaks instead of working until you drop. These five or ten minute breaks will help you stay mentally alert. These breaks can be used to stimulate different parts of your brain by doing activities like listening to classical music or taking a walk.

Speaking of walks, please don't overlook the aspect of physical exercise when trying to boost your brain power. Your brain is a hungry and demanding thing! It only makes up 2 percent of your body weight, but consumes 20 percent of your total oxygen and glucose stores. Your brain operates best when nutrient-delivering channels, like arteries, are kept clear. This is exactly what happens when you exercise.

Typically, the more fit you are, the faster your brain fires synapses responsible for quick thinking. Studies suggest that the brains of frequent exercisers process visual information more rapidly than the brains of more sedentary people.

Some quick brain-enhancing tips: Any activity that gets your heart beating faster will nourish your brain; learn a new physical skill that requires quick reflexes; or do something to throw your brain off. But don't get stuck in a routine of doing the same things day in and day out.

So far we have been discussing the brain in a very physical way. But what of the mind? The concept of mind is more intangible. We know that we have one, but where does it reside? Most experts at least connect the brain and mind, and many believe that they are one and the same. However the whole idea of the mind and consciousness is a fascinating mystery that we are going to take a quick look at in the remainder of this chapter. What is consciousness? It seems obvious, but it is perhaps the most baffling phenomenon associated with the human brain.

At the turn of the twentieth century, Sigmund Freud transformed the study of psychology into a modern science. In doing so, he proposed the first comprehensive theory of the human mind.

Freud believed that the mind consisted of two parts: the conscious and the unconscious. He believed the unconscious shapes behavior and is the repository of an individual's experience. Yet, Freud believed the ideas and drives of the unconscious could only be examined through creative outlets like dreams, fantasies or artwork.

Carl Jung, the eminent psychiatrist and disciple of Freud, took Freud's definition of mind one step further. Jung recognized both a conscious mind and an unconscious mind but felt that the unconscious had two categories:

1. An ever-changing personal unconscious made up of all the things happening to us that we are not paying attention to; and

2. A stable, collective unconscious made up of images, common to all humans, which influence and shape our lives.

Jung developed a fascinating theory called synchronicity which draws on the unconscious. Synchronicity pertains to oddly coincidental things popping up during a brief period of time. For example, you're discussing a movie you saw with a friend, you turn on the TV and the movie is showing. You then receive a phone call from the person with whom you saw the film. Jung felt that many of these coincidences may be engineered by forces at work on a personal and collective unconscious level.

William Kautz, an expert on intuition, looks at the mind as having three concentric circles: the inner core of our consciousness is surrounded by a larger circle of personal unconscious which, in turn, is encircled by the super-conscious which Kautz refers to as "the reservoir of all human knowledge and experience, actual and potential."[1]

We will look at Jung's collective unconscious as well as Kautz's superconscious mind later in the book. Much of the remainder of this chapter, indeed, much of this book focuses on your extraordinary unconscious mind. However, before we get into the unconscious, I want to introduce you to some exercises designed to enhance your senses and therefore expand your conscious mind. These exercises will also help you better understand the nature of this book. You are not just reading a book. You are taking part in an interactive experience! You are holding on to a workbook (hopefully you will think of it as a playbook) designed to truly fast forward your brain and to reach the outer limits of your mind! For you to receive maximum benefit from this book, you must try the exercises in this and the following chapters.

Developing Super Senses

Sight

Look at a photograph or picture for thirty seconds. Then, turn it face down so you can't see it. Next, list all of the details you can recall from the picture. Look again. Compare your notes with the actual picture. Identify what you missed and see if something comes to you about why you missed it. Note the differences.

Tracking the distinctions of an object increases the reality of the object. Your unconscious notices these things all the time. By practicing this technique you become more aware of the type of information your unconscious absorbs.

Sound

Listen to a recording of a song or speech. After the recording is over, use your keyboard, pen, pencil or cassette recorder, and write or record a detailed description about what you heard. Notice variations in the pattern of speech or the variations of the rhythms in the music you heard.

Notice the timbre of the sounds of the music or the speech. Notice the emotion that is being communicated and how it affects your feelings.

Notice if the words match the tone of voice. Detail everything that makes this recording stand out for you. Repeat the exercise, this time describing what you are hearing *as* you listen to the recording. Compare the two and determine which is better for you.

Evaluate if you hear more with your eyes closed or open. Sound stimulation usually increases if other senses are decreased. However, your retention will be increased if more than one sense is employed.

Listen to a television program, but don't watch it. Imagine the action taking place instead of using your eyes to watch. Base the action on what you hear instead of what you can see.

Tape what you are watching with your eyes closed, then go back and watch it with your eyes open. Compare the two. Which was more vivid? How do they compare?

When you are around others, begin focusing on the words you are hearing, not on what you are planning to say. Making active listening a part of your normal behavior will expand your conscious awareness.

Find a room with no distractions and notice the silence. Notice the natural sounds that take place around you: air conditioners, cars, the wind, birds, etc.

What sounds come to you when there are no artificial sounds—only silence?

Touch

Assemble an assortment of different shaped and textured items, such as: stuffed animal, plastic ball, glass, steel rod, wooden pencil, aluminum foil, screw, a variety of fabrics. Blindfold yourself or just close your eyes and pick up each item and explore it with your fingers. Picture the feelings in your mind as emotions. After you have completely explored one item, remove the blindfold or open your eyes. Write or record your sensations, detail by detail. The greater the diversity of your chosen items the better your results. Shutting down your other senses results in the refinement of the particular sense you are using.

Taste

It's nice to have an assistant for this one. Assemble an assortment of foods with different tastes and textures in bite-sized quantities, such as: fruits, vegetables, grains, dairy and sweets—cooked and uncooked. After you are blindfolded or after you have simply closed your eyes, your assistant will place one of the food items in your mouth. Explore the taste and textures. After you have completely explored one item, remove the blindfold or open your eyes. Write or record your sensations, detail by detail. The greater the diversity of your chosen items, the better your results.

Smell

Have an assistant help you with this one as well. Assemble an assortment of items, including the same kind of food items used above, plus non-food items, such as things you find in nature, and things manufactured that you don't usually associate with smell. After you are blindfolded or your eyes are closed, your assistant will place one of the items an inch from your nose. Inhale and explore your sense of smell. After you have completely explored one item, remove the blindfold or open your eyes. Write or record your sensations, detail by detail. The greater the diversity of your chosen items, the better your results.

If you practice the exercises detailed above you will begin to notice things that previously would have escaped your conscious mind. The more you practice the more refined your super senses will become. However, no matter how sharp you make your senses you still can't consciously take in everything.

The amount of information taken in by the brain each day is astounding. It has been estimated that the human brain makes over 100,000 operations per second and can hold 100 trillion bits of information. If our conscious minds tried to handle all of this, we would go crazy!

Every second, 100 million messages from our nervous system bombard our brain. Only several hundred are permitted above our brain stem and only a few of these receive some sort of response.

The human eye is capable of processing about five million bits of information per second. The human brain is capable of processing only five hundred bits of information per second. Think about those numbers and think about how much of that visual information you are aware of at any one point in time. And this is just what's coming in through one sense. You can't possibly consciously process all the information your eyes give you in one second, let alone all the information that you're given in a minute, an hour, a day, a week, a month, a year or a lifetime. In fact, it is estimated that in any given second we consciously process only sixteen of the estimated eleven million bits of information our combined senses pass to our brains.

Consider the cocktail party phenomenon. You're at a crowded, noisy party carrying on a conversation, the ambient noise all around you makes no sense and sounds like a gaggle of geese. However, if you cease your conversation and focus on the conversation between two other people in another section of the room, you can actually hear their words! All the conversations in the room are coming into your brain at one level. You just aren't aware of it consciously.

I was appearing in Saudi Arabia and the company hosting me had a farewell reception in my honor. It was a cocktail party (without the cocktails) and many conversations were filling the room. I was engaged in one of those conversations with a woman concerning the power of the unconscious. We tried the cocktail party phenomenon and focused on a woman and a man having a conversation across the room. They were talking negatively about the woman I had been conversing with, saying things like, "Can you believe what so and so has on tonight?" The woman was a little embarrassed but then we laughed about it. She then said, "You know I never liked that woman, but I could never figure out why. Maybe it's because she talks about me behind my back in social circles when I'm present and my unconscious picks up on it." Maybe.

With so much information bombarding our brain, much of it is ignored by our conscious mind. But that doesn't mean that the information is lost. Much of it is routed to the unconscious mind. The information is there, but the conscious mind does not always have direct access to it.

For example, you run into an old high school friend on the street whom you haven't seen in years. He remembers your name, but you can't recall his. You're embarrassed. You have a brief conversation and then walk away. As you are walking down the street, his name pops into your mind. This is an example of unconscious knowledge being tapped by the conscious mind. Here's another: Remember when you were taking a test in school and you read the question, but couldn't think of the answer, although you knew that you knew it? Maybe you went on to some other questions and then came back to that one and the answer was there. Or perhaps, you finished the test and as you were leaving the class-room and walking down the hall the answer came to you. Again, you had the information; it was in your brain. You just couldn't get to it when you needed to. Frustrating!

Have you ever awakened just before your alarm went off? Some people do this all the time. In fact, my friend, Bob Hendrik, went for years without wearing a watch and was never late for anything. We used to work together when I toured my stage show on college cam-puses. One day he was given a wristwatch as a gift. He grew dependent on the watch, and his inner sense of time faded although he still retains the ability to awaken right before his alarm goes off. Your inner sense of time, your "body clock," is another part of you controlled by the unconscious mind.

Think of the mind as an iceberg. The small portion of the iceberg visible above the surface represents the con-scious mind. However, the bulk of the iceberg lies beneath the surface and represents the unconscious mind. Your unconscious mind is a vast warehouse of knowledge, ideas and experiences. It's like a filing cabi-net filled with pictures of every person you ever met and every event that has happened to you. Obviously, if you could freely tap into this pool of unconscious knowledge you could make decisions with more insight, become more creative and be able to process new information in a much more insightful way. I believe your unconscious is really the key to tapping into your creative and intuitive capabilities.

Your unconscious mind is almost like a secret genius. There was an interesting article in *The New York Times* entitled, "Your Unconscious Mind May Be Smarter Than You."[2] The article focused on the work of psychologist Pawel Lewicki, who confirmed not only the existence and power of the unconscious mind but also how astonishingly smart it is.

In Lewicki's experiment, volunteers were asked to push buttons corresponding to the apparently random appearance of an "X" on a computer screen. The "X" was following a very complex but deliberate pattern based on ten interconnecting rules. As an incentive, the volunteers were told that they would be given one hundred dollars if they could figure out the pattern. None could. However, as they continued the test, each subject's response time quickened as they began to intuitively choose the spot where the "X" appeared.

In other words, their unconscious mind figured out the complex pattern although their conscious mind failed at the same task. It may sound unbelievable, but it's true! Your unconscious mind is not only smarter than you think, but it is smarter than you can consciously think!

In this chapter, I have given you a lot of information about your brain, your mind and how they function. I want you to be in awe of your mind! I want you to be thinking, "You mean I own a Rolls-Royce, but I'm driving a Buick!?"

I hope that I have already opened up your mind a bit to the fact that the mind has more possibilities than our ordinary modes of consciousness can imagine. Consequently, life has more possibilities than our daily experience allows. As life becomes more demanding, we need to explore those possibilities and it is just that exploration which awaits you in the chapters ahead!

2 | A Matter of Memory

A man's life is what his thoughts
make of it.

Marcus Aurelius Antoninus
(Marc Anthony, Roman Emperor)

I have made my reputation as an "extraordinist." Much of what I do in my role as a stage performer involves demonstrating what we term extraordinary phenomena (hence the name extraordinist). I'm talking about the types of phenomena that some people still refer to as the paranormal—ESP, mind over matter and the like. Many people, and perhaps you are one, don't buy into these concepts. So, this chapter will focus on a mental ability that we all have and that we can all recognize: memory. After reading this chapter, you should be doing extraordinary things with your memory—hopefully things that you wouldn't have thought possible.

Memory is really the vital source of all human intelligence. We couldn't do a thing, from creating great literature to tying our shoes, if our brain could not store and recall past experience.

No one really has a bad memory. If you feel that you do, what you really need to do is train your memory, and that's what this chapter is all about. We are going to delve into mnemonics—the art of memory enhancement.

Remembering something well hinges on three things:

1. Association: The more connections you make between new information and information already familiar to you, the better you can remember the new information. So, when there is something new or unfamiliar you need to remember, associate it with something you already know.

2. Interest: Generally, people easily remember what they want to remember. Retaining what they need to remember, on the other hand, doesn't have a great success record. You may know someone who can give you all the baseball statistics for all the players in the National League, but can't recall his mother-in-law's phone number. Often when you don't remember something, it's because you are not paying attention; you lack focus. Inattention and distraction are major factors that negatively affect your memory. With interest, your attention is easily focused. With focus comes clarity, and with clarity comes retention.

3. Repetition: The more you see, hear or practice that which you're attempting to remember, the greater your chances of remembering.

Let's practice a mnemonic technique right now in order to remember these three things. Think of the acronym AIR. A = Association; I = Interest; and R = Repetition.

Now, let's look at some ways to practice these techniques.

You read a book review and become interested in purchasing the book. To remember the title and author for the next time you are in the bookstore, imagine yourself buying the book and reading it. Strengthen the memory of where you are at the time you first read about the book. These steps force you to focus. Remember, lack of focus is your memory's greatest nemesis.

The next time you meet someone, and want or need to remember his or her name, begin to cultivate the habit of repeating the name back to the person as you are introduced. Often when you first meet someone your mind is not concentrated on the introduction—it's off somewhere else. Repeating someone's name requires concentration, and as a result you are more likely to remember the person's name the next time you see him or her.

Another technique is to use a person's name as often as possible during a conversation. You can also search your mind to find someone you know with the same first name, link the familiar person with the person you are being introduced to. Visualize them playing a game, engaged in a sport together or co-involved in a business or personal relationship. Now you have a familiar image to go with the name. Your mind should bring up this image when you meet that person again.

Another mnemonic technique would be to study the person and pick out an outstanding physical characteristic. Then associate their name to the characteristic. For example, I was working on a video project with a video editor named John. Simple name, but I always had trouble remembering it. This is very embarrassing for an extraordinist! John had a full beard. I visualized a toilet seat (as in "I've got to go to the john.") wrapped around his face in place of the beard. I never forgot his name, although if he ever shaved, I would be in trouble!

A man who occasionally waited on me at the post office was named Sam. I knew all the other postal workers' names, but often drew a blank on Sam. I started to visualize Sam in an Uncle Sam outfit, bending over the counter and giving me my mail. I never had the problem again.

It has been my pleasure to appear on a half dozen television programs with the dynamic duo of country and talk TV, Lorianne Crook and Charlie Chase of *Crook & Chase* fame. After one of my appearances, a staffer asked me for a memory tip to give audiences a way to know who is Crook and who is Chase. Apparently some people were confused! I said to visualize Lorianne dressed in a black cat burglar outfit and wearing a mask (burglar = Crook), she runs by Charlie, rips his mustache from his face and takes off with it. Charlie then chases (chases = Chase) her. The wild visual imagery of this and the association involved should guarantee that no one would again confuse the two.

Occasionally these types of techniques backfire. While appearing at a university in Maryland, I was to introduce the president of the group that sponsored my show. His name was Craig Pipenbring. I visualized me (Craig) throwing a pipe and my dog bringing it back to me. That night, from stage and in front of about five hundred people, I introduced him as Craig Pipenfetch! I'm only human!

In the Intuitive Edge workshops which I have conducted throughout the world, I always teach the following mnemonic system. In a short period of time, I have the workshop participants remembering an incredible amount of information by following the simple technique which I am about to introduce to you.

Following is a list of objects. Spend about thirty seconds reviewing them.

candle

car

house

dog

parakeet

beer

book

computer

peas

chandelier

lawn mower

necktie

castle

lake

motorcycle

screwdriver

Now, close the book and see what you can recall. Try to list the objects in order on a piece of paper. Once you've finished, come back to this page and begin reading the next paragraph.

How many did you get? Now, let's try it again, but this time we will use a mnemonic called the link system of memory. Using visualization, we will create a picture image that will link each object with the preceding one. Follow along with me: See a lighted candle; the candle is on the hood of a car; the car crashes into a house; the house falls over and lands on a dog; as the dog is flattened a parakeet flies out of its mouth; the parakeet lands in a glass of beer; the beer spills all over a book; a book falls off a shelf and lands on a computer causing it to explode; peas come flying out of the computer; the peas land on a chandelier; someone is trying to mow the grass using a big chandelier instead of a lawn mower; the person mowing the lawn gets his necktie caught in the lawn mower; see a giant necktie tied around a castle like a gift bow; the castle sits in the middle of a lake; you try to get to the castle on your motorcycle but it crashes; you try to fix the motorcycle using a large screwdriver.

Reread the paragraph and focus on the picture images. Then close the book again and try to recall all the objects in order.

Now, how did you do? You should find that with the help of the visual links created between the objects that you can remember them much easier. Since you are linking one object with another, you can go forward or backward through the list. You can even be given an object in the middle of the list, say chandelier, and remember the object before it (peas) and after it (lawn mower) because of the visual link.

You should make up some lists of objects or have a friend do it for you and practice the technique. As you begin practicing this, you'll discover that the more outlandish the picture image, the easier it is to remember. In theory, you can keep adding objects on and on, as many as one hundred or more. You must create your visual links as soon as the object is decided upon. In order for this technique to work, your list must be of objects, not concepts or other vague terms, so that you can create a visual image.

You may have trouble remembering the first object since there is no preceding object link. For this reason, we will borrow a mnemonic technique from the peg system of memory. In the peg system, a series of numbers are transformed into words. For example, the number one would equal gun. In the previous list, you might imagine someone shooting a gun to extinguish the flame of the candle. The object, candle, should then get you started on your total recall of the list.

Let's explore the peg system of memory for a moment and I'll show you how strong visualization plus association can be.

In order to get started, you must memorize the link between ten numbers and ten words. It's not hard at all as the objects rhyme with the numbers and the use of rhyming words is yet another mnemonic technique!

one = gun

two = shoe

three = tree

four = door

five = hive

six = sticks

seven = heaven

eight = gate

nine = wine

ten = pen

Once you have committed this list to memory, you will be ready to try the peg system. To show you how powerful this association process is, we are going to use a triple association! The number equals a peg word, the peg word is associated with yet another image and that image is linked to a specific name. Once you go through this, you have memorized, in order, the first ten presidents of the United States! Let's give it a try.

ONE linked to GUN: See a WASHING machine with GUNS spinning around inside! WASHING = WASH-INGTON.

TWO linked to SHOE: See an ATOM bomb being dropped, the ATOM bomb looks like a SHOE! ATOM = ADAMS.

THREE linked to TREE: See a CHEF's hat with a TREE growing out of it! CHEFerson = Jefferson.

FOUR linked to DOOR: See a MEDICINE cabinet's DOOR swinging open and MEDICINE falling out! MEDI-CINE = MADISON.

FIVE linked to HIVE: See a beeHIVE with MONEY stuck in the holes! MONEY = MONROE.

SIX linked to STICKS: See an ADAM'S apple with STICKS running through it! ADAM'S = ADAMS.

SEVEN linked to HEAVEN: See a car JACK jacking you up to HEAVEN! JACK = JACKSON.

EIGHT linked to GATE: See a VAN crashing into a big iron GATE! VAN = VAN BUREN.

NINE linked to WINE: See someone washing your HAIR with WINE! HAIR = HARRISON.

TEN linked to PEN: See ink squirting from an ink PEN all over a TIE! TIE = TYLER.

Read these over again in order to get the idea, and I bet that in no time you will have memorized the first ten presidents of the United States in order. Think of it this way: If I were to ask you who the fourth president was your mind should quickly think FOUR = DOOR = MEDICINE = MADISON! Or, if I were to ask you which president VAN BUREN was, your mind would connect VAN BUREN = VAN = GATE = EIGHT or the eighth president.

At first, these exercises may read a bit complicated, but I encourage you to put the techniques into practice. They really do work. Some people seem to pick up on the principle(s) right away and with others, it takes some time. I remember audiotaping these techniques for an infomercial product I created a few years ago. After one read-through of the sample link system and peg system lists, the audio engineer could recite everything backwards and forwards, and he said he thought that he had a bad memory!

I would like you to begin using these techniques as you go about your daily routine. A simple way you can begin is with a grocery list. The next time you get ready to shop, practice linking the items on your list. Or, when you have a series of things to do, use a double link. Think of a picture that represents each task on your "to do" list and link them all together. After a little bit of on-the-job practice, you'll find yourself doing things with your memory that you might not have previously thought possible.

Memory is an accepted mental capability. Developing a super memory is just a matter of obtaining some knowledge and learning the "trick" of applying it.

Remember the Rubik's Cube? Probably you, or someone in your family, owned one of these at one time. I was in high school when they first appeared and caused a sensation. Just in case you're not familiar with it, you have a six-sided cube with a different color on each side. You would scramble the cube, mixing up all the colors. Then, by twisting and turning it, you would try to get it back into its original, solved condition.

Dr. Rubik invented this puzzle to drive people crazy, and it worked! At first, no one could figure out how to solve it. Many people felt that it was impossible to solve.

They thought that once the cube was scrambled something happened internally which prevented it from ever returning to its solved condition. Then someone figured out how it was done, wrote an instruction book about how to solve the Rubik's Cube and people learned to solve it in a matter of minutes. On the old *That's Incredible* television show, I saw someone solve it using his feet!

The point here is that while something may look impossible (like a super memory) it probably isn't. Remember, nothing is impossible once you learn the "trick."

The mnemonic "tricks" you've learned in this chapter should really start you on your way to developing a super memory. There are really two benefits to this. First is the obvious benefits of a better memory. Second, you should ask yourself, "If I can do *this* with my mind, what else can I do?" You'll find out in the chapters ahead!

3 | Your Intuitive Edge

I did not arrive at my understanding of
the fundamental laws of the universe
through my rational mind.

Albert Einstein

Albert Einstein was an amazing individual.
Multidimensional in nature, he explored
ideas and concepts using his rational mind.
But his genius was his ability to trust those
moments of keen intuition, those flashes of
insight where ideas are born.

I like to think that everyone is exposed to
their intuitive natures from time to time. I
believe that Albert Einstein and other great
citizens of the world achieve their greatness,
in part, because of their ability to listen to
their intuitive minds.

I believe that each progressive step toward greater consciousness is a direct result of acting on a hunch, trusting our intuition. The impulse to engage is not driven by our rational natures. Action is a result of our creative hunches, our intuition, our unconscious mind. Like Albert Einstein, we can achieve things far greater than we ever thought possible simply by learning to first recognize and then trust our intuitive nature.

The wonderful thing about this is that as we go in search of our intuitive natures, we do not have to travel far. You see, it might be more accurate to say that most people simply don't notice their intuition. Our intuition is available to us at any time. We have simply learned to ignore it. We have grown accustomed to using our rational mind.

My hope is that this chapter will provide you with the key to open the door to an extraordinary journey, an exploration of another expression of self—a sixth sense called intuition.

The entire concept of intuition might be unfamiliar to you. So perhaps we should take a quick look at how others view intuition.

In his book *Paradigms,* Joel Arthur Barker said, "It is the ability to make good decisions with incomplete data."[1] This is a very direct assessment of what intuition can do for you. Baruch Spinoza, the seventeenth-century Dutch philosopher, concurred with Barker. He called intuition a "superior way of knowing ultimate truth without the use of prior knowledge or reason."[2]

American business philosopher R. Buckminster Fuller called intuition "cosmic fishing." Fuller said, "Once you feel a nibble, you've got to hook the fish." He said it was too easy to "get a hunch, then light up a cigarette and forget about it."[3] Learn to pay attention to your intuition when it speaks to you.

Ralph Waldo Emerson described intuition as "the primary wisdom." Saying, "In that deep force, the last fact behind which analysis cannot go, all things find their common origin . . . we lie in the lap of immense intelligence. We are the receivers of its truth and organs of its activity."[4] Now that is deep as well as powerful and true!

Texas billionaire H. Ross Perot encourages all of his employees to follow their instincts. Perot says, "Intuition is simply knowing your business. It means being able to bear on a situation everything you've seen, felt, tasted and experienced in an industry."[5] You would expect a successful and hard-nosed businessman like Perot to put something as intangible as intuition into these terms. Put this way, the idea of intuition doesn't sound "otherworldly" at all, but just sensible and practical. The other extreme can be found in psychologist Frances Vaughan's definition of intuition: ". . . a way of knowing . . . recognizing the possibilities in any situation. Extrasensory perception, clairvoyance and telepathy are part of the intuitive function."[6] While some of you may be uncomfortable with Vaughan utilizing "paranormal" terms in her definition, I, for one, believe that developing your intuition will allow you to experience other abilities that used to be referred to as paranormal, but are now called extraordinary phenomena or EP. We will look at these abilities later in this book.

William Kautz, an expert on intuition who heads up the nonprofit Center for Applied Intuition, became interested in the intuitive process while researching creativity. He found that breakthroughs were not the result of rational thinking, although that aspect of mind did play a role. Kautz's research showed him that almost invariably scientists who discovered great breakthroughs did so in a flash. "This told me that there had to be some process going on in their minds that was generating information—not just reprocessing information already received. That process of direct knowing is intuition."[7]

Richard Feynman was a wonderful scientist who helped chart the course of modern theoretical physics. He came to international attention when he explained, in layman's terms, why the space shuttle Challenger exploded. Feynman had the uncanny intuitive ability to look at long mathematical equations and instinctively know if they were correct or not. He said he could "feel" if the flow of the numbers was not quite right.

I think of intuition as a primitive skill that early humans relied on. Primitive peoples roamed the planet guided and protected by a well-developed "sixth sense." Through the centuries, humankind relied less and less on intuition. This important sixth sense started to disappear. It is not entirely gone, but in many it lies deep beneath the surface. You see, today the trend is to promote logical thinking at the expense of intuition. And, by the same token, some people who do develop their intuitive capabilities tend to overreact and rely on them too much. It is best to seek a happy medium. Children seem to find this balance naturally. It is only as they grow and mature that their intuitive abilities are downplayed.

Oftentimes, we overemphasize rationalization and facts, reason and logic. We need to rid ourselves of these obstructions at times to allow us to tap into our intuitive capabilities. Logic and analysis can only take you so far. I encourage you to combine them with an intuitive leap to become really successful and learn to open the door to greater possibilities.

You have to eliminate the concept that intuition is some kind of supernatural magic. It is a perfectly normal and natural mental ability that we can use. Intuition can help you solve problems, make the right decisions, come up with creative ideas and even forecast the future. It can ensure that you are in the right place at the right time. This is the "intuitive edge." It can be a vital element in your business and personal life. Stop for a moment and think how successful you would be if you fully used your intuitive edge. If activating your intuition only increased your effectiveness by 10 percent, your world would be drastically different.

While intuition is hard to pin down, there have been some interesting studies exploring this extraordinary ability and how it relates to the business world.

Roy Rowan of *Fortune* magazine conducted surveys and interviews among the CEOs of Fortune 500 companies and found that the vast majority of these people not only believed in intuition, but admitted to using it in their business careers. Remarkably, while they acknowledged intuition, many hesitated to call it that and preferred to label their intuition a gut feeling, business instinct or simply a hunch. But it is really the same thing. Rowan elaborates on these fascinating interviews with these titans of business in his excellent book, *The Intuitive Manager*.

Henry Mintzberg reported on a large study he conducted with corporate executives in the *Harvard Business Review*.

Mintzberg found that successful, high-ranking managers operating under stress and pressure constantly relied on hunches and feelings when faced with complex problems that the rational mind could not handle. Mintzberg concluded that managers could be most successful by combining logic with intuition.

At the New Jersey Institute of Technology, parapsychologist E. Douglas Dean and engineer John Milhalsky spent ten years studying the relationship between business executives' intuition and their businesses' profitability. In one test, CEOs guessed a randomly generated one hundred-digit number. The remarkable finding was that 80 percent of the executives whose scores were above average in intuition had also doubled their companies' profits in the previous five years.

In a similar study at the University of Texas in El Paso, Weston Agor tested the intuition of two thousand managers and discovered that the top-level leaders scored higher on intuition than those ranking lower in the corporate structure. In a follow-up study of seventy executives, Agor found that all but one admitted using intuition, although they were reluctant to admit it to their colleagues.

Ray Kroc owned an industrial kitchen-supply company in Chicago. In 1952, a San Bernardino drive-in restaurant run by Richard and Maurice McDonald caught Kroc's attention because of the number of milk-shake machines they were buying. Kroc entered into business with the McDonald brothers and created a franchise that, within five years, consisted of 228 McDonald drive-ins across the country.

However, Kroc was getting less than 2 percent of the restaurants' gross earnings—a quarter of which he had to give to the brothers. So in 1961, Kroc offered to buy the brothers out. The brothers told Kroc what they needed: $2.7 million and that they wanted to keep the original restaurant. This was an exorbitant price at that time. Kroc's lawyer advised him against it, and Kroc himself was furious over the amount. Kroc said "I'm not a gambler and I didn't have that kind of money, but my funny bone instinct kept urging me on. So, I closed my office door, cussed up and down and threw things out the window. Then I called my lawyers and said, 'Take it!'"[8] Needless to say, Kroc's funny bone instinct paid off and was one of the most lucrative intuitive decisions in business history.

In 1906, Wall Street wizard Jesse Livermore acted on his intuition and sold his Union Pacific stock. He did this despite the fact that the company was in great financial shape. A few days after Livermore sold his stock, the great San Francisco earthquake hit. Union Pacific suffered incredible losses of equipment and train track. As a result, Union Pacific stock plunged. Livermore ended up netting more than $250,000 (the equivalent of over $3 million today) because he listened to his intuition.

Kevin Parry, one of Australia's leading entrepreneurs, freely admits that he uses his intuition. Parry goes as far as saying that he can not think of a single major venture that he went into without checking his intuition first.

Estée Lauder, founder of the giant cosmetic company, was famous for her intuitive ability to pick bestselling perfumes. Apparently, she could out-predict market research every time. Her son said that he could happily spend millions of dollars on a certain investment without market research as long as he had his mother's agreement and intuitive backing.

John Marion was the chairman of Sotheby's North America, the famous auction house. He was also known as the greatest auctioneer of the twentieth century. He was so in demand that few of Sotheby's other auctioneers ever got a chance to handle a major auction. Marion partly attributed his success to intuition. Marion referred to his intuitive feelings as a super-awareness. This super-awareness allowed him to "sense" where the next bid would come from. He would then focus his attention on that section of the room, drawing the bid out. He couldn't explain how he knew, but he was very successful and his success gave him supreme confidence to the point that he felt as if he was in total control of the bidding process.

Some very interesting stories of applied intuition come from the area of law enforcement. Here's just one example: In 1997, the biggest armored car theft in U.S. history was pulled off. A nationwide manhunt ensued for the accused suspect, Philip Noel Johnson. Johnson was arrested at an international bridge on the Mexican border after Customs inspector Virginia Rodriguez got a "funny feeling" about him.

Johnson was on a bus with twenty-five other passengers. On a hunch, Rodriguez asked Johnson for identification. She was given a driver's license with a fake name on it. Customs ran the license and discovered that the name was an alias Johnson was known to be using. Customs spokeswoman Judy Turner praised Rodriguez's work as "fabulous." "He [Johnson] acted ordinarily in a lot of ways, but she [Rodriguez] had an intuitive feeling and followed through on it. Sometimes it's just someone's tone or failure to make eye contact that tells a Customs official to ask more questions."[9]

Another explanation for Rodriguez's interest in Johnson may have been the wanted poster with his photo on it in the Customs office. Johnson had drastically altered his appearance and all the Customs officers agreed that it would have been nearly impossible to pick him out of a lineup based on the photo. However, I believe that Rodriguez's intuitive mind could connect the photo of Johnson to Johnson in person. That, combined with other subtle clues picked up unconsciously, could have directed Rodriguez to Johnson.

In most of my workshops, I share this story and my theory as to why Rodriguez was attracted to Johnson. I then try to find a "Virginia Rodriguez" among the participants. I get someone on the platform who has been successful in some of the previous intuitive tests that were conducted. That person is handed a padlock and four nearly identical looking keys. The person tries all four keys in the lock and finds that only one key opens the padlock. The keys are mixed and then placed in front of the participant. The person is then asked to choose one key without thinking about it, using intuition as his or her guide.

Eighty percent of the time the volunteer selects the one key in four which opens the lock! I can then point out the physical difference in the key which opens the lock from the other keys. Once I show the person the difference, the conscious mind recognizes what the intuitive mind knew all along.

Going back to the business world, hotel magnate Conrad Hilton was famous for his "Connie's hunches." Here's an example: During a sealed bidding process for the Stevens Corporation, Hilton entered his first bid at $165,000. He said about the incident, "Somehow that didn't feel right to me. Another figure kept coming, $180,000. It satisfied me. It seemed fair. It felt right. I changed my bid to the larger figure on that 'hunch.'"[10] Hilton's bid proved to be the highest—but by only $200! Hilton's intuition won the bid and eventually netted him more than $2 million on this one deal.

Hilton described his intuitive process by saying that he would work through all the logical planning and then wait for an internal response. "When I have a problem and have done all I can to figure it, I keep listening in a sort of inside silence till something clicks and I feel a right answer."[11]

I used Conrad Hilton's intuitive formula myself recently when buying and selling a house. I still live in the same city that I was born in. One summer while home from college, I delivered phone books for the telephone company. My delivery route took me to areas of the city I had never been in before. While making one delivery, I came upon my dream house. It was a beautiful Tudor home on about five acres of land. Since making that delivery, I always wanted to live in that house. I got married about four years later. I used to drive my wife, Charlotte, by the house, and she fell in love with it as well.

About twenty years after I made that phone book delivery, the house came on the market. At the time, I couldn't afford it, but Charlotte and I went to look at it anyway.

Then we waited. We studied the local real estate market, looked at other homes and did all the analytical, market research. At this point, I used Hilton's intuitive method. I internalized all the information and waited for the right answer to come to me. A figure popped into my mind. The figure was 25 percent less than the original asking price for the home. I waited until my intuition told me that it was time to contact the real estate agent and to make a bid. I followed my intuitive mind and made the bid when my intuition told me to. The bid was accepted!

Now, I already owned another home which I then had to put on the market. I followed the same procedure, letting my intuition speak to me. I came up with an asking price for my home. The price that my intuition said was right was 15 percent more than experienced real estate agents told me I could get for the home. Next, I decided when I should try to sell the home. Intuition led me to choose a Sunday in August as the right time. I took a photo of the house, ran it in that Sunday's paper and sold the home, for my asking price, in two hours to the third couple who viewed it! My intuitive edge saved me over $115,000 on the two transactions. This is just one example of how I put my intuition to work in my everyday life. You can do this, too!

I am sure you have experienced your intuitive mind speaking to you. For example, have you ever met someone and instantly felt you couldn't trust this person? Or, does this seem familiar: You are about to do something and then an inner voice tells you not to. In retrospect, you found that you should have listened to that inner voice. The reverse could also be true: You make up your mind not to do something and then that same inner voice encourages you to "go for it." You do, and you are successful. This feeling, this inner voice is your intuition. We all have a built-in protection system which guides us and keeps alerting us to potential problems.

In the past, you probably experienced intuition in a random manner. In fact, you may have heard the term a "flash" of intuition. Because it is just a flash, a temporary feeling you "sense" but then it leaves, you tend to ignore it because it is fleeting and makes no sense to your rational mind. However, if you recognize it, give it credence and deliberately try to access it, your intuition can then give you many more details of a given situation.

It is common for people to have natural intuitive abilities in a certain area of their life. Some are particularly intuitive when it comes to family and friends. Some people are highly intuitive in business. Some only seem to access their intuitive skills when the situation involves other people and can't seem to make their own intuition work for them on a personal level. However, if you spend a little bit of time working on it, I believe that you will find intuition playing a role in all areas of your life.

How do you develop your intuitive nature? One of the most basic things you need to do is create a sense of awareness of your intuitive side. To help you do this, I've put together a quick test you can take which will indicate your natural intuitive ability.

Intuition Self-Assessment Test

Answer yes or no to each of the following questions.

1. Have you ever had a premonition (either when asleep or awake) of an unexpected event which later occurred?

   ❏ Yes   ❏ No

2. Have you ever (either when asleep or awake) been aware of the thoughts or experiences of another person which later proved true?

   ❏ Yes   ❏ No

3. Did you ever hear the doorbell ring and instantly know, for no apparent reason, who was ringing the bell?

   ❏ Yes   ❏ No

4. Do you ever answer the phone knowing, for no apparent reason, who is on the other line?

   ❏ Yes   ❏ No

5. Have you ever been thinking of a person only to meet him or her unexpectedly?

   ❏ Yes   ❏ No

6. While playing cards, wagering or in business, have you ever had a "lucky hunch" which proved correct?

   ❏ Yes   ❏ No

7. Have you ever had the feeling that a letter or some form of communication was about to arrive from some particular person and it did?

❏ Yes   ❏ No

8. When something was lost, did you ever have the sudden feeling that you knew where it was and were right?

❏ Yes   ❏ No

9. Have you and another person ever said the exact same thing at the exact same time?

❏ Yes   ❏ No

10. Have you ever noticed a seemingly insignificant topic or idea that seemed to follow you, coming up again and again throughout the day in conversation, reading, etc.?

❏ Yes   ❏ No

11. Have you ever shivered, felt depressed or sad for no apparent reason only to find out later that something negative had happened at about the same time?

❏ Yes   ❏ No

12. Have you ever come across a person, place or event that was entirely new to you but you had the feeling that you had experienced the moment before?

❏ Yes   ❏ No

13. Have you ever felt someone staring at you and been correct? Or, have you ever stared at someone until they "felt" your gaze?

❑ Yes   ❑ No

14. Have you ever been lost in your own thoughts to the point where you lost track of what was happening around you?

❑ Yes   ❑ No

15. Do you have vivid dreams?

❑ Yes   ❑ No

16. Have you ever found yourself singing or humming a song and then turned on the radio and heard the same song playing?

❑ Yes   ❑ No

17. Has the solution to a problem ever come to you in a "flash" of insight?

❑ Yes   ❑ No

18. Do you often know the correct time without consulting a clock? Or, do you often awake just prior to your alarm going off?

❑ Yes   ❑ No

19. Have you ever been singing or humming a song only to find out that a friend has had the same tune running through his or her mind as well?

❑ Yes   ❑ No

20. Have you ever known, for no apparent reason, what was in a letter or package without opening it?

❑ Yes   ❑ No

Total your number of "Yes" responses and rate yourself using the table below:

0-5 "Yes" responses: You tend to rely more on your normal five senses and may be very skeptical of anything you can't see, feel, hear, touch or smell. To become more intuitive will require concentrated effort on your part and perhaps a shift in your belief structure.

6-10 "Yes" responses: You are on the verge of discovering your intuitive abilities. You are probably open-minded to the fact that intuition is an ability that we all have and can be further developed.

11-15 "Yes" responses: Whether you realize it or not, you probably use your intuitive powers on a daily basis, often relying on intuition.

16-20 "Yes" responses: You're a natural "intuit" and are probably already aware of the importance intuition plays in your life. You have a high degree of ability that can be harnessed for tremendous growth.

Your intuitive mind will benefit if you spend some quiet time alone. It gives you a chance to think about things. Your creativity is also best served by spending time alone. I believe intuition and creativity are linked.

Mozart is a wonderful example of a highly intuitive and creative composer. He wrote: "When I am, as it were, completely by myself, entirely alone, and of good cheer—say, traveling in a carriage, or walking after a good meal, or during the night when I cannot sleep; it is on such occasions that ideas flow best and most abundantly. Whence and how they come, I know not: nor can I force them."[12]

The history of the creative arts and sciences is full of accounts like Mozart's. Authors have felt that they were not actually writing the book themselves, but that some force took hold of the pen and wrote the book through them. Artists have started painting something with no idea of the eventual outcome and end up painting masterpieces. Scientists have had the answer to a nagging problem "pop" into their heads as if someone placed the thought there.

You might say that these people were geniuses and that your mind doesn't operate in the same way. But everyone is intuitive and everyone can think like a genius. Some people seem to take to this way of thinking more naturally than others but everyone can develop intuitive thinking and make better use of it in order to enhance their lives.

If geniuses like Mozart and Einstein used intuition to achieve some of their greatest accomplishments, why doesn't everyone want to use intuition? Many people do use it, but don't wish to talk about it. Some fear being ridiculed if they told anyone about their intuitive thinking. Part of this problem has to do with Western culture. There are people who use intuition very successfully, but they always back up their intuitive ideas with facts and figures.

Although the intuitive thought came first, the facts help these people explain their conclusions in a logical manner.

Once you acknowledge your intuitive nature, the next step is to activate it. First, you must learn to be still and relax. Create a quiet mind as it were. The meditation and relaxation exercises in this book are a perfect way to begin accessing your intuition. It doesn't take long to carry out the exercises and you will not only benefit by heightening your sense of intuition but also by reducing stress. There is nothing like utilizing a relaxation and mind-focusing technique to revitalize you, making you sharp and effective for the rest of the day.

As you relax, develop the conviction that your intuitive mind has all the answers. Consider a specific problem, think it over in a detached, dreamy manner and ask your intuitive mind for the answer. Be confident that your intuition will work for you. Remember this line from the film *Field of Dreams:* "If you build it, he will come." If you focus your intuitive mind on a problem, the answer will come.

You must develop patience. Incredible intuitive insights don't necessarily come as soon as you ask. You have to remain relaxed and confident. The answer could pop into your mind when you least expect it. You might be strolling through the grocery store when the answer to your problem surfaces. Or, it may come to you over your morning cup of coffee, or as you begin to fall asleep at night, or as you awake in the morning.

I find that I often get an answer when I'm relaxed and not consciously focused on my problem or question. I spend a lot of time on airplanes and driving a car. I may be staring out an airplane window, looking at clouds at thirty-five thousand feet, when the answer comes. I may be driving down a seemingly endless, flat country road, and the solution to my problem will hit me right between the eyes! Hiking is one of my favorite activities. When I'm out alone in nature and my blood is pumping, I often get an intuitive insight into a problem in my life. I am also ready to listen to my intuitive mind. If something comes to me while I'm on an airplane, for example, I write it down. I often carry a small pocket recorder and record ideas as they come to me. I have made paying attention to my intuitive mind a priority.

I remember taking a seven-mile hike one morning in a rain forest on the Olympic Peninsula in Washington. Idea after idea came to me, but I had no recorder or method to write down what my intuitive mind was telling me. So, I linked the ideas together using the mnemonic techniques described earlier in this book. When I got back to my lodge room, I immediately wrote everything down and practiced mind-mapping techniques to expand on all the ideas. It was an incredibly productive morning that resulted in the premise and outline for another book.

I always remain confident that my intuition will work. Part of the reason for this confidence is past experience. My intuition has served me well in the past and I believe it will continue to serve me well in the future.

Despite the fact that there are so many accounts of people's intuition really paying off for them and despite the studies which have been conducted proving the value of intuition, there are still skeptics. It is crucial that you get rid of any skeptical attitudes you have about your intuitive abilities. Why? Because we are dealing with the intuitive mind which is connected to the unconscious. Your unconscious mind knows how you really feel about something. Your belief in intuition and all its possibilities must not only be a conscious decision on your part, but you have to believe in it on an unconscious level as well. You can trick your conscious mind into believing something, but your unconscious is impossible to fool—it knows how you really feel.

To help you get over any skeptical attitudes, think back to a time that your intuition worked for you. You may have decided to do something on the spur of the moment, for no logical reason at all, and whatever you did really paid off. Or you may have had an impression about someone which proved correct. Think back to a time when you didn't follow your inner voice, and you should have. Try to come up with many examples of these types of occurrences. Relive these incidents in your mind. This will help strengthen your intuitive connection. Start right now to begin to notice these intuitive flashes as they happen to you in your life, no matter how trivial they may seem.

When your intuition speaks to you, you may act on the information immediately. Or, you could do as some people do and start using your logical mind to gather information that supports your intuitive decision. The important thing is that you pay attention to your intuition and act on the impressions that come to you. Your intuitive mind must realize that you are taking it seriously! As you pay more attention to your intuition, intuitive flashes will come to you more frequently.

While you should take these intuitive insights seriously,

you shouldn't become too serious concerning developing your intuition. By that I mean don't try to force it. Don't approach it with a do-or-die attitude. A playful attitude will help more than anything. Despite the fact that many of the problems you will consult your intuition about will be serious ones, a sense of humor will help you connect with your intuition. Try to have fun with your intuitive exercises.

Is your intuition infallible? Of course not! Don't think that I am telling you to forget about analytical thinking. If you are accustomed to a rational thought process, continue using it. All the information that you gather through your logical mind can help your intuition. The more information your mind has on any level, either consciously or unconsciously, the more effective your intuition will be. But don't be afraid to go off on tangents as you try to connect with your intuition. Don't lock yourself into a set pattern of behavior.

As you begin contacting your intuitive mind, you may only get a "sense" of what it is trying to tell you. It may seem like a feeling of awareness just beyond the reach of your conscious mind. When this happens, don't ignore it, but don't try to rush it either. Simply be aware that your intuition is speaking to you and be confident that, in time, the entire answer will be revealed. Don't analyze what is happening and don't try to make sense out of what may only be a partial intuitive insight. You will know when the entire intuitive impression is revealed because it will "feel right." Remember, intuition is an intangible thing. Once the impression feels complete, you can then start analyzing what your intuition is trying to tell you and how it applies to your current situation.

Your intuitive abilities are heightened by the addition of any and all information. For example, in a situation where another person is involved, face-to-face communication is a better way to feed your intuition than a phone conversation. Likewise, a phone call is better than a written letter or an email. Why? Because our unconscious mind constantly processes things like body language and voice inflection. It is very easy for someone to lie to you in an e-mail. It is much harder for them to get away with it during a phone call or during a face-to-face meeting. You don't have to know anything about body language for this to work. It can work for you on a totally subliminal level. You might say that highly intuitive people are super-sensitive on a subliminal level.

You can feed your intuitive mind by constantly feeding your conscious mind with new experiences and new information. You never know what bit of information your intuitive mind can use. Your intuition appreciates everything, and it sometimes makes surprising connections with seemingly unrelated pieces of information.

My wife, Charlotte, is an antiques dealer. She doesn't specialize in one particular area and in the world of antiques there is so much to know and so many different categories to be familiar with. Charlotte reads all she can on the subject as a whole. She goes to as many antique shops as she can, and she looks at everything. What she observes and consciously remembers is, of course, beneficial to her business. However, she can also tap into all the information stored in her unconscious as well. Oftentimes she makes a shrewd buy at an auction based on an intuitive insight that she had which had to do with long-forgotten information she picked up somewhere.

When seeking intuitive guidance, it is important to be specific as to what you want your intuition to tell you. If you are trying to be successful in your career, don't ask your intuition how to become the CEO of your company. Take it in steps. How can you be successful in a current project you are working on? What must you do to sell to a specific client?

As you begin utilizing your intuition to reach your goals, you will find that your intuitive mind can help decide the right goals for you. There have been cases where people in business have left successful yet stressful careers to find a simpler, happier life based on intuitive insights. Often, what we think we want is quite different from what we really need in order to live a happy and productive life. Your intuition can certainly point you in the right direction.

As you begin to discover what you really need and want out of life, focus on those goals. Write them down and think about them. This feeds your intuition. Be open to change. As we grow, our goals can and do change.

If you have a problem, write it down. This clarifies it and makes it concrete. You can then combine your intuition with a mind-mapping exercise to help solve your problem. Write down everything that pertains to the problem and every possible solution, no matter how ridiculous it may seem. Don't censor anything. As you write, a sudden flash of insight may come to you as it did to Archimedes when he yelled "Eureka!" More often than not, this won't happen, but writing all this information helps impress the ideas on your intuitive mind so it can get to work and provide you with the answer when it is ready.

For intuition to operate at an optimum level, a period of incubation is usually needed. Dreams and meditation, examined in other chapters of this book, are ways to let your mind incubate.

Once you start connecting with your intuition on a regular basis, you may start questioning whether or not your intuitive insight is "real" or correct. As I said before, intuitive feelings are not infallible. Sometimes they are there for you in black and white and are absolutely correct. Occasionally, they might be completely wrong. Or they may seem too "out there," so you choose to ignore them and then later find out that you should have paid attention to the intuitive thought. There are things you must consider when trying to analyze your intuitive thoughts in an attempt to ascertain whether or not they are "real."

Is your intuition telling you something you don't want to know? We tend to shy away from bad news, but this is an area where your intuition can be particularly helpful. You may get an impression that a personal relationship is about to end. You don't listen to your intuition and you spend more time in what proves to be a dead-end relationship.

Occasionally, you may second-guess your intuitive thoughts because you feel guilty about them. For example, let's say you have always had a distrust of lawyers. You view them as a necessary evil. You then find yourself in a situation where you must work with an attorney, and you instantly and instinctively have a strong dislike for this person. You may write the feeling off to your prejudicial attitude toward attorneys or to a negative experience in your past, and proceed to work with the individual. In other words, you don't listen to your intuition. Many times in situations like this, you will find out later that your intuition was correct and you should have listened to it.

Some people don't want to act on their intuition because they don't want to be put in the situation of explaining why they did something when they have no logical reason to support it. Some people are embarrassed talking about using their intuition. However, I am convinced that if everyone talked about how often their intuition was right, we, as a culture, would develop a greater awareness as to just how powerful intuition can be.

Intuitive thoughts are sometimes so out of line with our traditional way of thinking that we ignore them. This is a trap you must not fall into. Intuition and imagination are linked.

An example of an unimaginative person who probably never accessed his intuition is Simon Newcomb. In 1903, Newcomb was president of the National Academy of Sciences. This traditional-thinking scientist made the grand announcement that man would never be able to fly. Newcomb felt that the proof that flight was impossible was irrefutable. The Wright brothers flew at Kitty Hawk that same year!

Conversely, Edwin Land was a very forward-thinking inventor who accessed his intuition and defied the constraints of traditional thinking. Land was walking along a beach with his daughter, and he took a picture of her. His daughter asked why they couldn't see the photo immediately. Land used this event to jump start his brain and he created the Polaroid camera which, by the way, was turned down by the traditional-thinking Eastman Kodak Company.

We can also expect too much from our intuition. All the information we require may not be available to us intuitively, and our intuition may only provide us with a piece of the puzzle. However, always make use of what insights you do receive and be grateful for them. If we only have a piece of the puzzle, we may need to do some interpretation as to what our intuition is trying to tell us. It is not uncommon for someone to put the wrong interpretation on an intuitive insight. You must be careful. For example, you sense that your best friend is trying to avoid you. Your intuition tells you that he is trying to do something behind your back. You put a negative spin on this and later find out that he was planning a surprise birthday party for you. He was indeed doing something behind your back but it was a positive thing, not negative at all.

Don't underestimate yourself. Your intuition may tell you that big things are in store for you, perhaps a big promotion or a big sale to a particular company. Your conscious mind, on the other hand, tells you that you don't deserve these things, or you aren't capable of this kind of success. I had an intuitive feeling that I would appear on *The Tonight Show with Jay Leno* and that I would write a book. These intuitive thoughts were sometimes hindered by my conscious thoughts that "television people" would never pay attention to a guy from West Virginia or that a publisher would never find my writing of interest. More often than not, your intuition knows what you are truly capable of.

Are you afraid of taking a risk? Some intuitions require that you take a certain amount of risk. If they prove wrong, you could end up with egg on your face. You must learn to be comfortable with taking a certain amount of risk. Taking a risk is sometimes the only way you will get ahead. Risk-taking keeps you involved and excited, and oftentimes it is very rewarding. Not taking risks causes you to become stagnant.

Once you get an intuitive impression, take a good look at it. Combine your intuitive information with information gained through logic and reasoning. This should help you verify your intuition. Everyone should have a support system of friends and advisors. Please feel free to discuss your intuitive ideas with others. Get their opinions. After you have examined the possibilities from every angle, make your decision.

However, even those who are perceived as "experts" are not always right. In 1973 the prime minister of Israel, Golda Meir, had a strong feeling that war was about to break out. Her advisors provided her with convincing evidence that she was worrying about nothing. Meir put her feelings to rest. A short time later, the Syrian and Egyptian armies attacked Israel. Many Israelis were killed. Meir was in shock. She couldn't forgive herself for not following her intuition and relying on the opinions of others instead.

If your intuitive feeling is strong and persistent, I would be inclined to follow it, even if the experts say otherwise. Remember Ray Kroc's funny bone instinct.

Many creative artists describe the creative process in a very detached way. I believe they are describing the way their intuitive minds speak to them.

For example, Henry Miller was suffering from writer's block while working on *Black Spring,* the final volume of his *Tropic* trilogy. He had been blocked for two days; he couldn't write a thing. As he looked through one of his notebooks, one line jumped out at him and intuitive inspiration was ignited. Miller described it this way: "It is about ten in the morning when this line shrieks at me. From this moment on—up until four o'clock this morning—I am in the hands of unseen powers. I put the typewriter away and commence to record what is being dictated to me. . . . This continues and continues. I am exultant and at the same time I am worried. If it continues at this rate I may have a hemorrhage."[13]

Miller tried to escape the grip of this creative surge by going out to dinner and leaving his notebook at home. It didn't work. He covered the tablecloth with writing! Miller said, "Someone is dictating to me constantly—and with no regard for my health."[14] It didn't stop until after four in the morning—an eighteen-hour rush of creativity—and at that point Miller became "a free man again."[15]

Larry Gelbart wrote ninety-seven episodes of the classic *M*A*S*H* television show. He also wrote the film *Tootsie* and the play, *A Funny Thing Happened on the Way to the Forum.* Gelbart is obviously an incredibly funny and creative writer. He describes the creative process behind his comedy writing this way: "I don't ask for it, I can tell you that. It's like your brain is somebody else, just using your body as an office."[16]

Puccini claimed that the music of *Madame Butterfly* was dictated by God. He said he was just an instrument for recording it all. Mozart said his music came from his Divine

Maker. The German composer Wilhelm Richard Wagner believed it was clairvoyance. Pëtr Tchaikovsky credited it to his "guest." In a letter, he said that no effort of mind was necessary. No effort of conscious mind perhaps.

Tchaikovsky said, "It is enough to obey one's inner voice, and if the former of the two lives [outward-material] does not suppress with its depressing incidents the second, artistic, one, then work progresses with absolutely unbelievable speed. Everything is forgotten, the spirit throbs with an absolutely unbelievably and inexpressibly sweet excitement, so that before one has time to follow this impulse somewhere, time has passed literally unnoticed. There is about this state something somnambulistic."[17]

Tchaikovsky also knew what it was like to create in a state of exaltation and exhaustion, similar to Henry Miller's. He said, "It is useless trying to find words to describe to you the unbounded sense of bliss that overcomes me when a new main idea appears and begins to take definite form. I forget everything, I behave like a madman, trembling and shaking in every limb, with scarcely time to jot down the sketches, so quickly do thoughts pursue one another. If that state of the artist's soul which we call inspiration and which I have tried to describe to you, should continue uninterrupted, it would be impossible to survive a single day. The strings would snap and the instrument shatter to pieces! Only one thing is essential: that the main idea and the general outline of all the separate parts appear not by means of searching, but of their own accord, as the result of that supernatural, inscrutable and wholly inexplicable force which we call inspiration."[18]

In more modern times, 1997 to be exact, country music

diva Dolly Parton retreated to her childhood home, a cabin in the Appalachian mountains, in order to write some original songs. Parton said, "Once they [the songs] started rolling, I could not stop. I just got going and it seemed more and more intense as I went. Finally, it just built up to where I had a major climax. It felt so good I wanted to have a cigarette afterward."[19]

Parton's marathon song-writing session resulted in her first collection of original music in years. The critics raved over her *Hungry Again* CD. Not only did she pen enough original material for one album, but she wrote a total of thirty-seven songs during her writing marathon in the mountains. She recorded all of the songs—enough to fill three albums.

Pablo Picasso said: "Painting is stronger than I am; it makes me do what it wants."[20] He also said that at the start of any work "there is someone who works with me."[21]

These are just a few examples of creative people who used their intuitive minds in extraordinary ways. These artists didn't seem to seek out their intuition, it took hold of them. These artists were all passionate about their work. Perhaps that is why their intuitive minds spoke to them so clearly and so easily.

I encourage you to be passionate about your life and your life's work. Life is far too short to spend time doing what you don't want to do. You can make your life anything you want it to be. If you live your life passionately, you will ignite your intuition. People who go through life uninvolved miss out on so much, including their intuitive natures.

Expect your intuition to be there for you. Combine

your logical mind with your intuitive mind. Your intuition can provide you with so much. It can help you in business and in your personal life. Your intuition can protect you from making bad decisions and it can put you on the right track. Your intuition can be the doorway to your creative self.

Intuition speaks a universal language, communicating through the portals of conscious awareness: sight, sound, taste, smell and touch, as well as through the unconscious. Intuition communicates through our imaginations and realizations.

You have your own best form of intuition. It is always there for you. You can call it, as Ray Kroc did, your "funny bone instinct." You may wish to refer to it, as Conrad Hilton did, as a "hunch." Or, you may favor John Marion's "super-awareness" description. But, regardless of what you call it, I hope I have shown you how to trust and use your natural intuition. I hope that you will start using it today.

Look at it this way: Your life is a result of the decisions that you make. You owe it to yourself to make full use of your mind when making those decisions and not just the tip of the iceberg. Use your intuitive edge and enhance your life in every possible way.

4 The Extraordinary Mind-Body Connection

We are what we think. All that we are arises with our thoughts. With our thoughts we create the world.

Gautama Buddha

A good friend gave me a poster while I was in college. I kept it on my wall for years. It said, "Only those who can see the invisible can do the impossible."

To me, it was all about visualization. An Olympic weightlifter sees the bar over his head before he lifts it. A martial arts expert sees his or her hand through the board before striking it.

Brain training is all about the roles the brain plays in every physical action of the body. Sport psychologists say that if we want to do something well, we must control the way the brain works during the endeavor. Mentally living through a specific physical activity prepares the brain for the real activity.

Some brain trainers believe that you must not only visualize the activity, but also see yourself being successful in it. Golf great Jack Nicklaus never hits a shot, whether in competition or practice, without having a clear picture in his mind of just what he wants the shot to look like. Similarly, track star Carl Lewis always focused on the end result of his task, the successful completion of it, before the attempt. Olympic gold medal diver Greg Louganis "mind scripted" each dive an estimated forty times. Sometimes, he "saw" the dive at normal speed and sometimes in slow motion.

You can mentally rehearse or visualize any task, not just athletics. Before I begin any project, I take the time to sit down and imagine how I want things to go. Often this process allows me to "see" trouble spots before they arise. Sometimes the information given through visualization is uncanny.

Let me give you an example. Before each of my performances, I actually "live" the presentation twice. Once in my mind and once on stage. One time, while trying to visualize an actual show before it happened, I had an image of a person on stage with me. I was about to begin a demonstration wherein I "levitate" a table with the help of an audience member. In my visualization, I asked the woman to put her hands on the table. When she brought her arms out from behind her body, she had no hands— they just weren't there! This startled me. I had no idea why I saw this, but it alerted me to that portion of my program. When I actually came to that particular demonstration in the performance, the woman who came on stage was missing her left hand! Since she had to use her hand in the demonstration I was prepared or forewarned for what normally would have been a complete shock to me and a potentially embarrassing situation.

An American prisoner of war was held captive in Hanoi for seven years during the Vietnam war. He was an avid golfer before going off to war. In order to keep his sanity while in prison, he played a round of perfect par or scratch golf on his favorite course every day in his mind. He played under every type of adverse conditions, wind, rain and the like. Shooting par on this course was a goal that he had never accomplished in real life, but he visualized and reached it every day in his mind. Upon his release and return to the United States, one of the first things he did was to go to this golf course. Although he hadn't held a golf club in over seven years, he went out and shot par that day for the very first time in his life. He had been mentally rehearsing this round of golf for seven years.

Science increasingly supports mental rehearsal. It has become popular among athletes, especially golfers. What the results indicate is that to the unconscious mind there may be no difference between what is real and what is vividly imagined.

A psychological study was carried out concerning the ability of a basketball player to make a foul shot. Groups of players were recruited and their skill at making foul shots was tested and recorded. The players were then split into two groups. The first group spent an extra thirty minutes a day, after their regular practice session, shooting from the foul line. The second group spent thirty minutes after practice sitting in a dark room and imagining themselves shooting foul shots. This was an exercise in guided visualization. The players created vivid mental images of themselves and their foul-shooting techniques. At the conclusion of the testing period, all the players were retested to see if their skills improved. The group who actually shot foul-shots for an extra thirty minutes a day showed a slight improvement. However, those who only visualized shooting foul shots showed a dramatic increase in skill.

Positive visualization can be your best technique to help you reach your full potential. Use the three Vs: Visualize, Verify and Verbalize. Visualize what you want and how to get it. Verify what needs to be done in order for you to achieve it (for example, can you do it on your own? Do you need the help of others?). Verbalize: Tell people about it and put action to your thoughts.

For many, this will involve a change in thinking. You begin to function from the end result. In other words, you see yourself successful before you are successful. You start at the end! And when I say visualize, I mean bring in all your senses. Really get into it. Imagine not only the sights, but the smells, sounds, tastes and feelings of success and peak performance. And when you reach your goal don't forget to reward yourself and to be thankful.

Psychologist Mihaly Csikszentmihalyi came up with his "flow theory" in the 1970s. To him, the flow is a state of intense concentration akin to ecstasy. It is purely natural and while it lasts, it improves your mental and physical performance. Chess masters, long-distance runners and musicians have all experienced it.

In children, the flow manifests itself the most. Children can play imaginary games forever. The older we get, the less we can focus on one single activity. Csikszentmihalyi says to recapture that childhood feeling of flow we need to match whatever activity we are involved in with our skill level. Action merges with awareness, your attention becomes completely centered and you enter the flow. Tasks greater than your skills create anxiety, and when your skills exceed the task boredom sets in. So match your task to your skills. Screen out distractions, get comfortable and focus on the task. Eventually, you may lapse into a spontaneous distraction-free state that is a main catalyst for the flow. Csikszentmihalyi says that you can't experience it on a full-time basis but, if you work at it, you can enter the flow several times a day with durations from a few minutes to hours at a time.

As an aid in reaching the flow state, you may want to try meditation. University of Chicago studies in brain-wave patterns seem to link the flow-state experience with meditation, which we will be looking at later in this chapter.

A by-product of the flow is the extraordinary phenomenon of "elongated time." It is the ability to see fast moving events in slow motion. Pat Haden, former NFL quarterback, describes elongated time this way, "In the pocket, it seemed like you saw 150 yards of the field. The receiver was bigger than life—you didn't see the defenders."[1] To this day, Haden enjoys watching slow-motion replays because it reminds him of his experiences of elongated time.

Michael Jordan describes it like this, "The rim seems like a big ol' huge bucket."[2]

John Olerud of the Toronto Blue Jays says, "When things are going well, there seems to be more time to react to a pitch. And it doesn't matter what that pitch is. It's just that it feels like you have more time to react."[3]

Golden State Warrior's player, John Starks says, "It's like you see something before it really happens."[4]

How can this be? Don Clifton, chairman of Gallup Inc. and the man who coined the term "elongated time," speculates that the eye can take about sixteen pictures a second. He believes that people who experience elongated time are taking fifty or sixty pictures a second and thinks that they have the nerve tracks to make this possible.

All of the examples we have looked at so far demonstrate the mind-body connection. We have primarily looked at this connection from a task-oriented view and spent a lot of time on athletics. However, it goes much, much deeper. The mind, the brain and the immune system are physiologically linked.

An individual's beliefs and expectations can set off an internal healing process. How? Placebos, be they beliefs or sugar pills, have been associated with the brain's endorphins. When placebos are successfully applied, the brain's anxiety signals to the body decrease. This combination enhances a sick person's well being and might allow that person's natural recovery mechanisms to function better.

In the 1950s, a man with life-threatening cancer took an experimental drug called Krebiozen. It was being touted as a "miracle cure." After one dose, his tumors went into fast and later complete remission. This same man then heard reports that Krebiozen was not the miracle drug he had thought. The tumors came back almost immediately! His doctor saw what was happening and gave him what he referred to as a "new and improved" Krebiozen. There was no such thing, the doctor simply gave him water. The tumors went into remission again! The man then heard that Krebiozen was declared worthless by the FDA and that there was no "new and improved" version. He died a few days later!

Another man was watching his eight-year-old son whittle. The boy cut himself, severing the arteries in his left wrist. The father grabbed the boy and together they concentrated on the blood and yelled, "Blood, you stop that!" The bleeding stopped, and in an abnormally short time the wound healed!

While I hope you are never in the situation that this boy and his father were in, I do know that you will experience pain of one kind or another in the future. The next time you're in pain, try the following techniques for pain control.

1. Establish the reason behind the pain both physical and mental.

2. Disassociate yourself from the pain. Visualize it outside yourself or within a little box in one area of your body. This gets you away from the "I feel bad all over" syndrome. View the body part in pain as an inanimate object.

3. Distract yourself from your pain. Watch a movie, read, talk with someone about positive things. Don't dwell on your pain.

A study among people sixty five years and older showed that those in poor health who felt they were in good health had a better chance of surviving than those in physically good health who believed they had poor health!

Consider this: During World War II in Nazi concentration camps, one experiment involved discovering how fast people would starve to death. The prisoners were given only three hundred calories per day. In one camp, most of the inmates died as a result of this diet, except for one small group. When liberated, the leader of the group revealed their survival technique. The group would sit and talk with one another. They would describe the best meals they had ever had and do so in great detail. They would truly relive the meals, "smelling" the aromas, "tasting" the fine food and doing so with only the power of their imagination. This indicates that the brain can receive information about weight from sources other than food. One study showed that people who just saw a sizzling steak increased insulin production which increased fat into their cells which, in effect, would cause them to gain weight!

Remember the experiment involving rats described in the first chapter that demonstrated the fact that the rats' brains could physically grow when given the proper environment? Here's another extraordinary rat experiment. Scientists injected rats with saccharin water followed by a drug causing temporary illness. Eventually just injecting saccharin water caused the rats to be sick. It also worked in reverse. A group of rats were given an immune-boosting drug and then were made to smell camphor. Another group was given a drug inducing temporary illness while smelling camphor. Soon, just the smell of camphor alone either increased the rats' immune systems or caused the other group of rats to become ill. The rats' brains told their immune systems what to believe based on past experience and what they were now conditioned to believe.

All that we've discussed thus far in this chapter demonstrates that what we believe about ourselves directly impacts our health. There is so much to learn about the brain and how it relates to our health. Future discoveries concerning the brain may change medicine, as we know it, for all time.

The Quiet Mind

What lies behind us, and what lies before us are tiny matters compared to what lies within us.

OLIVER WENDELL HOLMES

I mentioned meditation earlier in this chapter and what follows is a series of meditation, relaxation and visualization exercises that I hope you will enjoy. From earlier chapters, you know how busy your mind is. These exercises "quiet" your mind to make it more receptive to what your unconscious mind and your body are trying to communicate.

Meditation is an aid in becoming receptive to the connection between the conscious and the unconscious and between the mind and the body. It simply removes outside distractions and helps you become more in touch with yourself. The idea is to reach an extreme state of physical calmness which results in a sharpening of mental focus and allows you to dip into your unconscious storehouse. We slip into this state often, however we usually refer to it as daydreaming.

There are four primary brain-wave levels:

1. Beta, which is a rapid state of consciousness that exists as people are speaking, for example.

2. Alpha, which is a level of alertness slightly less than beta.

3. Theta, or drowsiness.

4. Delta, or deep sleep.

Meditation involves focusing on a single mental task in order to achieve peace of mind. When in a meditative state your metabolism, heartbeat and breathing slow down. Electrical waves produced by the brain alter from beta to the smoother alpha waves or even theta which translates into a state of peaceful alertness. All this represents a mild altered state of consciousness.

It takes time to become adept at meditation. However, if you practice the following, you will begin to experience what meditation feels like:

1. Make sure your environment is shut off from outside distractions and any bright lights eliminated. Make sure the temperature of the location is comfortable to you.

2. Focus your eyes on a single point like a candle flame or a specific pattern on a piece of wallpaper.

3. Stare at this point and concentrate solely on it.

4. You may have better luck with a nonvisual way. Breathe slowly with your eyes closed and count each

time you exhale. The regulated breathing becomes your focus and the counting keeps your thoughts diverted from anything other than the task at hand.

Other techniques include that of Nikola Tesla, the famous inventor. He would recite poetry as a centering technique. Charles Darwin regularly used daydreaming for inspiration. J. P. Morgan played a hand of solitaire prior to any important business decision in order to focus his mind.

I am going to give you some relaxation and visualization "scripts." I would like you to record these or if you have a friend with a particularly soothing voice try to get them to do it for you as they are written in the third person. Either way, here are a few suggestions to follow when making your recordings:

1. Practice first! Try to get the script down so that you don't stumble as you read it and so that it sounds natural as you make your recording.

2. Speak slowly. Go at about a third of your normal rate.

3. Allow plenty of time for any instructions to be followed.

4. Your speech should sound natural, but also a bit monotonous and repetitious in order to be most effective.

5. Try to do each recording in one take with no starts or stops. This causes the exercise to really flow and therefore be much more effective. Don't get frustrated as this will probably take several tries (how many times did it take you to get that answering machine message down pat?), but it will be worth it.

The tapes you create from the scripts in this chapter will aid you in focusing, reducing stress and feeling better about yourself. I suggest you play them on a regular basis. Play them before trying the other exercises in the book. Take note to see if your success rate improves after playing the tape and quieting your mind before attempting the exercise as compared to when you just jump into the exercise "cold turkey."

You may wish to set aside a special time each day to play these tapes. You may want to start your day with one of the exercises. You may find one that is particularly effective to listen to at night just before going to sleep or another might really get you focused before taking on a big project or right before a big meeting. Personally, I like to listen to these tapes in the morning before I begin my activities. The tapes put me in a more powerful frame of mind to accomplish my objectives.

You may also want to try these tapes when you have a question. Ask yourself the question before listening to the tape. Then let it go. The question will seep into your unconscious. When the recorded exercise ends, the thoughts that come to mind may very well contain the answer to your question.

These exercises are designed to break the train of conscious thought. In this way, you bypass your conscious mind and become familiar with the images created by your inner mind. The exercises will free you from the potentially destructive distractions that can inhibit developing your intuition.

Script Number One

Begin to breathe from your diaphragm, just below the stomach. Concentrate solely on breathing. Focus on your breathing. As you focus on your breathing begin counting each exhalation from one through ten. Take slow, deep breaths. Tell your body to relax. Ready, one ... two ... three ... four ... five ... six ... seven ... eight ... nine ... ten.

Now we're going to do this counting from one through ten again. Remember, count each exhalation from one through ten. With each breath your body is becoming more and more relaxed. Take slow, deep breaths. Your body is relaxing. Ready, one ... two ... three ... four .. five ... six ... seven ... eight ... nine ... ten.

We're going to do this counting one more time. The third time, counting each exhalation from one through ten again. And remember, slow, deep breaths. With each exhalation your body becomes even more relaxed. Ready, one ... two ... three ... four ... five ... six ... seven ... eight ... nine ... ten.

Now just feel your breathing for a few minutes. You feel very relaxed, a very soothing feeling. Very pleasant. Now bring your consciousness back to the real world.

Script Number Two

Close your eyes and take three deep breaths. One ... two ... three. Consciously think of relaxing all of the muscles in your body. Begin with your head, feel the muscles in your head, neck and shoulders begin to relax. All the tension stored there is leaving, slowly melting away.

Feel this relaxing energy move into your chest and arms. Feel a pleasant warmth drifting into the relaxed muscles.

Down into your stomach now. Relax those muscles. Your fatigue is leaving, being replaced by soothing, relaxing energy.

That same powerful energy moves into your legs and feet. Your muscles are relaxing. Nice, pleasant warmth drifting all through your body from your head to your feet.

I want you to take some nice, gentle breaths. Become aware of your breathing. When you feel ready, slowly open your eyes and bring your attention back to the real world.

Script Number Three

I want you to squeeze your eyes shut as tightly as you can as I count to three. Ready? Begin. One . . . two . . . three. Keeping your eyes closed, relax.

Now, I want you to tense all the muscles in your right arm for my count of three. Ready? Begin. One . . . two . . . three. Relax those muscles. Relax your right arm.

Now, we are going to do the same to your other arm, your left arm. Tense all the muscles in your left arm. Ready? Begin. One . . . two . . . three. Relax the muscles of your left arm. Think of yourself relaxed.

Now, I want you to form your hands into fists. Clench them tight. Ready? Begin. One . . . two . . . three. Relax your hands, think of yourself relaxed.

Now, we're going to move into your stomach muscles. Tighten your stomach muscles. Ready? Begin. One . . . two . . . three. Relax. Relax your stomach muscles.

Now, stretch your right leg out in front of you. Tighten all the muscles in your right leg. Ready? Begin. One . . . two . . . three. Relax those muscles. Relax the muscles in your right leg. Think of yourself, relaxed.

Now, I want you to do the left leg. Stretch your left leg out in front of you. Tighten those leg muscles. Ready? Begin. One

. . . two . . . three. Relax the muscles in your left le
yourself, relaxed.

Slowly open your eyes. Welcome back.

Script Number Four

This is my personal favorite. It is the work of
Richard Webster of New Zealand. Richard is a true
Renaissance man. He is an accomplished author, lec-
turer and performer and has greatly influenced my
life. I thank him for the permission to use this wonderful affirming visualization and relaxation exercise
in this book.

Close your eyes. Feel your eyelids getting heavy. It is a
pleasant feeling. Become aware of your breathing. Notice
how every breath makes you more and more relaxed. It's so
peaceful and quiet and relaxing and you are drifting
deeper and deeper into a beautiful, calm, tranquil state.
Each breath is becoming deeper, it's becoming easier and
easier to do. Just feel the relaxation coming in with each
breath and allow the stress and tension to flow out each
time you exhale.

I'm going to ask you to take three deep breaths. As you
breathe in, imagine all sorts of pleasant energies coming
into your body, making you feel vibrant, healthy and alive.
And as you exhale, imagine all the negativity and stress in
your life coming out and disappearing forever.

Take the first deep breath. Good. Pleasant energies coming in and negativity floating away. That's good. Very good.

Second deep breath. Vibrant health and enthusiasm
coming in. Negative thoughts and feelings disappearing.

Third deep breath. Feel those good energies coming in
and allow the negative ones to go. You don't need them

anymore so let them go. They are no longer a part of your life. You no longer need them. Let them go. Just enjoy the pleasant relaxation. Let it spread through every nerve, muscle and fiber of your body. So pleasant, so relaxing. You're just drifting and floating deeper and deeper with every easy breath. Just enjoy it. Let pleasant feelings flow throughout your body as you get more and more relaxed with each breath you take.

And in this nice, calm, pleasant, relaxed state, just become aware of what a miracle you are. You are a miracle. You are a miracle of nature. You have unlimited potential. You can do anything. You can climb a mountain, travel the world, become anything you desire. Picture your intuition, your potential. See all of humankind being interconnected. Because of this, you can communicate with anyone. You can access any knowledge. You can sense the future. Yes, you are a miracle and you can do anything. You absolutely have the power and the ability to develop your potential just as far as you wish.

To help you achieve this, you will find that you can quickly relax whenever you wish. It will become easier and easier to do. Easier and easier to do. See yourself calm and relaxed and at ease with your potential. You are starting an incredible adventure that will enhance all of your abilities. You will unleash all that potential that has not yet been utilized. You can do it. See yourself in your mind's eye operating at peak performance. You are a success at whatever you try. And every time you succeed congratulate yourself, and it will spur you on to develop and grow even further. You can do it because you have unlimited potential.

Now, in just a moment, I will count from one to five. When I reach five you will open your eyes feeling fine and refreshed. You will be invigorated and full of energy. But you will still be able to get to sleep easily tonight. In fact, you will sleep particularly well. Now, we are coming up on the count of five.

One, gaining energy, feeling just fine.

Two, mind keen and memory perfect, remembering absolutely everything that transpired during this peaceful meditation.

Three, looking forward to a vibrant future as the person you know you can be.

Four, almost there now. Becoming more and more aware.

Five, eyes opening and feeling fine, relaxed, alert and ready to go.

Script Number Five

Close your eyes. Relax. Tilt your head back as though you were looking at an object just above eye level. Now, imagine a hot summer's day; feel the heat. It's a comfortable heat, pleasant, radiating throughout your body.

See a sidewalk. Steam rising off it. Someone dropped an ice cream cone on the sidewalk. See the ice cream cone on the sidewalk. It's your favorite flavor. See the color of the ice cream. Sense how it would taste.

Now, take three deep breaths with me while still visualizing the cone. One ... now take the second deep breath, still seeing the cone ... good, very good. While still visualizing the cone, I want you to take the third, deep breath with me ... good.

Now, begin to breathe naturally; continue your natural breathing. Continue to see the ice cream during this time. Watch it become soft as it melts in the gentle heat of the summer sun.

Continue your natural breathing, as the ice cream cone continues to melt, running a bit on the sidewalk. Continue your breathing. The ice cream cone is melting more rapidly, getting smaller and smaller.

With each breath you take, more and more of the ice cream is melting onto the sidewalk, slowly becoming a pool of flavor. Your breathing continues. The ice cream continues to melt. See the ice cream totally melt. It is spread out all over the sidewalk.

Now, I want you to take five deep breaths with me. Your eyes still closed. One . . . good, very good. Two . . . three . . . number four . . . and five. . . . Feel how relaxed you are. Now, open your eyes and be aware of the thoughts that enter your mind.

Script Number Six

[**Author's Note:** While I have received a great deal of positive feedback on the following script, if you are claustrophobic you may want to skip it!]

Close your eyes. Relax and tilt your head back as though you were looking at an object just above eye level. You are outside on a bright, sunny day. You are enjoying nature, walking through the woods. See yourself in this setting. Through the trees you see an opening. What appears to be a cave. You are going to explore this cave.

Now, take three deep breaths with me—one . . . two . . . three. . . . Begin breathing normally as you walk up to the cave's entrance. You are still in the bright light of the sun. You have a flashlight with you. You take it out, turn it on and enter the cave. Light still filters into the cave from the outside. Your flashlight is creating a powerful beam of light which illuminates the path before you.

Breathe naturally, continue your normal breathing as you start to descend into the cave. Now the light from the outside is fading. Your flashlight is still powerful. It is lighting the way in front of you.

I want you to begin to feel safe in this space, this cave, as if this place is the final destination of a long journey. It's a place you want to be. You are curious and excited but you have no fear.

Continue breathing normally as you descend deeper and deeper into the cave. The beam of your flashlight is starting to get weaker. It's getting dark around you, but you have no fear. This is where you want to be. Where you need to be. With each breath you take the light is getting more faint. It's getting darker. You're descending deeper and deeper into the cave. You can barely make out the walls of the cave around you, but you still feel safe. You have no fear.

Continue breathing normally as you begin to reach the bottom of the cave. You're now there. You have descended all the way down to the end of the cave. You are where you want to be. You have ended the journey. You are in total darkness, but you are totally comfortable. You see nothing but blackness all around you but you are at peace.

While you are here in this dark, safe place, take five deep breaths with me. Number one . . . good . . . second deep breath . . . blackness all around but safe and at peace . . . number three . . . no fear . . . number four . . . safe and relaxed and at peace . . . number five.

Now, keep your eyes closed. See the blackness, but begin to notice your thoughts. Stay in this state for as long as you want. Just relax with your eyes closed and continue to notice your thoughts. And when you feel like it, open your eyes.

I can't encourage you enough to put these exercises on tape and to practice them. If you would like a copy of these exercises professionally recorded by me, see the information on contacting me in the back of this book.

As you practice these exercises you are experiencing other forms of consciousness. The better we learn to apply other forms of consciousness in our lives the more enhanced our lives will become.

The Intuitive Pendulum

The mind of man is capable of
anything—because everything is in it,
all the past as well as all the future.

Joseph Conrad

Whatever you do, do not skip this chapter! You will learn all about a fascinating device that will help you communicate with your intuitive mind. You will have a tool to help you get in touch with your unconscious mind in a very direct, physical way. Several of the chapters that follow will incorporate the device you will construct as you read this chapter.

When I introduce someone to the idea of intuition, I use the pendulum as a starting point. In fact, when I conduct my Intuitive

Edge workshop for business people, much of the focus is on the pendulum. You see, much of what we call intuition is intangible. It's a feeling, a sensing. With the pendulum, you have visible proof of your intuitive mind communicating with your conscious mind, you can see it happen.

The history of the pendulum stretches far back in time. There is evidence it was used in the ancient cultures of China, India and Egypt. It is, after all, a pretty simple concept. There is no great technology behind it. Indeed, a written or even a spoken language is not needed to operate it. This is why even the most primitive of cultures have used pendulums.

The fact that the pendulum has something to offer can be evidenced by its use through the ages. From the tribal shaman who used a piece of carved bone tied to a strip of leather to find the best hunting grounds, to soldiers in Vietnam who used them to locate hidden explosives and underground tunnels, to prospectors who try to find water and precious minerals by utilizing the pendulum.

My uncle first introduced me to the pendulum when I was fourteen years old. To me, it was like magic. My uncle could locate hidden water supplies or a hidden object. He found lost objects and many other wonderful things all via the pendulum.

You may already be familiar with the pendulum. One of the most common uses in recent times seems like an old wives' tale. A pregnant woman suspends a sewing needle by a strand of her hair over her palm. The ring then swings in either a circular direction or back and forth in a straight line. If the pattern is circular it is supposed to indicate that the unborn child is a girl; if it swings back and forth in a straight line, this indicates a boy. Pendulums were sold as "sex detectors" for this very purpose at one point in time.

I first seriously experimented with the pendulum when I was in my mid-teens. I instructed my high school girl-friend in the operation of it and she was very intrigued. She became quite proficient with it, particularly when it came to "guessing" the sex of an unborn child. She acquired quite a reputation for her newfound skill and pregnant women constantly asked her to tell them whether they would have a boy or a girl. One time she attempted to tell a young pregnant woman the sex of her child and the pendulum wouldn't move at all. The three of us thought it strange, but we didn't give it much more consideration. The woman miscarried!

I want you to be serious about your pendulum work. If you are, you will have far more success with it. Although there are many fine ready-made pendulums available for purchase, you may want to construct your own special pendulum. Indeed, the time spent finding and choosing just the right materials and working with them will not be wasted at all. The act of constructing your pendulum is an exercise in creativity all its own.

In taking an active and serious interest in constructing your pendulum, your creative energy almost becomes a part of the pendulum itself! Hopefully, your appetite is whetted and we can get on to the business of making your personal pendulum.

Your first decision will involve the material from which you will make your pendulum. Some people favor natu-ral materials like seashells, rocks, crystals or wood.

However, the choice of things you can use is limited only by your imagination—rocks, gems, wooden shapes, bone, shell, tiny bottles, rings, etc. I saw one man use a brass bell hung from a leather thong. Another man used his key chain suspended by a string. A pocket watch and chain would work for the right person as would a long, dangling earring. I have also seen people use only a chain with nothing suspended from it.

During one of my workshops, a woman wasn't having much luck with the pendulum supplied so she began to use the tassel of her corded belt and got immediate results.

The most unusual pendulum I ever saw was that of a young woman who had a long, braided ponytail which hung below her waist. She would swing the ponytail over her shoulder and hold it at her fingertips. The end of her hair would swing in any direction!

One of my favorite pendulums is an antique ring I inherited from my uncle, suspended on a silken cord. The ring is eighteen-karat gold and cast in the form of a coiled cobra snake! It has two small rubies for eyes and a diamond on its head. It is both beautiful and mysterious, and it always causes much comment whenever I use it in the presence of others.

You should have fun searching for just the right object to use. Let your creative and artistic self go! Why not find something truly unusual, beautiful or dramatic?

If you are looking for an inexpensive easy-to-find pendulum, go to a sporting goods store and buy a one-ounce fishing sinker. You can get a sinker in the shape of a pyramid which works extremely well or in the more traditional teardrop shape. This pendulum can serve you well until you create your "perfect pendulum."

Small, lightweight pendulums usually respond more quickly than heavy ones. However, don't rule anything out. Create pendulums of different sizes and weights. There are times when you will have more success with one pendulum than another. Go with your intuition, and try not to analyze why this is so.

Once you have that special object to use for your pendulum, you then need to suspend it from something. In many ways, your choice in this matter is as important as your choice of the object you are trying to suspend. You can use all sorts of materials. Again, if you are after a natural look, you may want to use cotton or silk thread. If you make that trip to the sporting goods store for a sinker, pick up some light fishing line as that works well as does heavy carpet thread. You may want to use a watch chain or a jewelry chain. At one time, I bought children's bracelets sold in craft stores—just a simple chain with a clasp. I would attach the clasp to a fishing sinker for example and have a ready-made pendulum.

Currently, I favor a cord that you can get in any craft or fabric store. They come in a variety of colors with either silver or gold metallic thread interlaced with one other color. The use of this easy-to-find and inexpensive cord makes repairing your pendulum simple should the end become knotted or frayed. Whatever you end up using, your pendulum needs to be suspended by about six inches.

If you use some type of fabric to suspend your pendulum, you will want to double-knot it at the point it attaches to the pendulum. Then put a spot of super glue or nail glue on the knot so that it doesn't come undone. You will also need to dip the end of the fabric in clear fingernail polish to keep it from becoming frayed.

How will you carry your pendulum? You can find small leather and velvet bags designed to carry jewelry which would work well for your pendulum. You might also consider a small ring box although it could prove too bulky if carried in your pocket. A small bag is really the recommended way to go. Unless of course, you already wear a medallion of some type which you can use as a pendulum. This way it is always with you, suspended about your neck.

In fact, the first mass-produced pendulum that I was involved with was a crystal prism which came in a small silk bag. The crystal was suspended by a loop of black cord. This way you had the choice to wear the pendulum around your neck either inside or outside of your clothing or carry it in the bag.

If you would like a specially made pendulum, similar to the one that I currently use, see the information on contacting me at the back of this book.

Now, let's put that pendulum to use!

Sit at a table and hold the pendulum by the end of its string with your elbow resting on the table's surface. Will the pendulum to move. Don't try to get it to move by conscious physical force. Relax and in an easy way just concentrate on movement. The pendulum will either swing back to front, side to side or swing in a circular motion either clockwise or counterclockwise. Some people have almost immediate success; others will take longer. The point is to take whatever time you need to explore and make the connection.

Our first step in doing something practical with the pendulum is to give meaning to the motion. The chart included in this chapter will help. Hold the pendulum over the chart, above its center, not quite touching the paper. Ask yourself a simple question for which you know the answer. For example, in my case, I might ask, "Is my name Craig?" Note the direction of the pendulum's swing. It should move forward and back along the yes line. Think of it as if you were nodding your head up and down to signify yes.

Now ask a question (for which you know the answer) which would result in a no response. Again, in my case, I might now ask, "Is my name Jeff?" The pendulum should now move from side to side, indicating a no response, as if you were shaking your head no.

The reason we do this preliminary test is to illustrate how the pendulum works and to establish how the pendulum's swing reacts to you. In other words, your own responses might be the opposite of what I just cited. Front to back for you might mean no, while side to side could mean yes. The pendulum may also respond in a circular pattern, either counterclockwise or clockwise. It doesn't matter how it responds. It only matters that you get two distinct movements: one response for yes and one for no. It is important for you to establish your own set of swing patterns.

When working with the pendulum, you should not force answers out of it, but allow it to answer as it wishes. Your state of mind should be alert and ready but passive.

The Intuitive Pendulum Chart

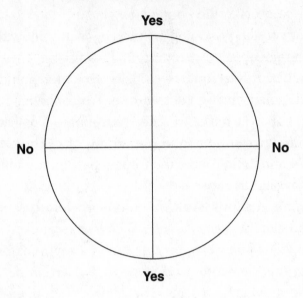

Practice willing the pendulum to move in different directions, constantly answering questions to which you already know the answer. After you have worked with the pendulum in this manner, your inner mind will have learned its lesson. The swing patterns will be set.

So, how can this thing work? It is nothing supernatural as some people previously thought and surprisingly still do! The answers come from within you!

When you operate the pendulum, you experience mind over matter, in a sense. It is a mind-body connection called *ideomotor response:* ideo meaning idea and motor meaning motion. Your unconscious sends signals to your body to control the swing of the pendulum. The unconscious thought creates a physical reaction.

A more common example of ideomotor response would be this: You're driving down the interstate and running very late for an appointment. You think to yourself, "I'm going to be really late, I've got to get there." All of a sudden you look at your speedometer and find yourself going ninety miles an hour. Your unconscious is saying, "If we have to get there, let's step on it!" Consciously you feel yourself exerting no extra pressure on the gas pedal. Your unconscious has taken control of your physical actions.

Once you get proficient with the pendulum you can get into questions that you don't consciously know the answer to, but your unconscious might. It can even be used to analyze your inner feelings, thoughts and emotions!

One of the most practical uses of the pendulum is locating lost objects. When you lose something, 90 percent of the time it's because you placed it somewhere but can't remember where. That is you can't consciously recall, but your unconscious may very well know the answer.

While holding the pendulum, ask yourself a series of questions pertaining to the lost object. For example, you might start by asking if the object is in the house. If you get a no response, you then start to ask if it is at other locations that you visited since you last remember having the object in your possession. If you get a yes response when asking if it is in the house, you then ask if it is in the bedroom, working your way through the rooms of the house until you get a "yes." You then narrow the room down into sections. For example, you might ask, "Is the object near the doorway? Is it in the nightstand?", etc. In this way you can actually track down a lost object.

Let me give you a personal example of locating a lost object. I was in Fort Lauderdale, Florida, over a three-day period. I was scheduled to make one appearance a day at each of three branch campuses of Broward Community College. On the evening of the second day, the student leaders in charge of my appearances asked me out to dinner and a movie. One of them, Archie, picked me up at my hotel. We had a great time, but the next morning when I started to leave for my third and final appearance I couldn't find my rental car keys. I looked all over the hotel room. No keys. So, I got out my pendulum. I asked, "Are the keys in the hotel room?" No. "Did I have the keys with me last night?" Yes. (This was actually a surprise since on a conscious level I thought I had left them behind when I went out with the students.) "Did I leave them at the restaurant?" No. "At the cinema?" No. "Are they in Archie's car?" Yes. I called Archie and asked him to look in his car for the keys. He found them, brought them to my hotel and I was off! The really interesting part of this story was that the keys had to have fallen out of my pocket as I was sitting in Archie's car—a fact that I wasn't consciously aware of (remember, I believed that I had left the keys behind in the hotel room the night before). My unconscious mind was aware of the physical sensation of the keys leaving my pocket and knew just where they were. Following the same procedure, you might be amazed to see what "lost" objects you can recover.

You can ask the pendulum any type of question. From the very personal ("Am I afraid of having a close relationship?" or "Am I in the right job?"), to the very practical ("Is this statement true or false?" or "Should I call on client X today?").

As you experiment with your pendulum, you will notice that you only need to get a slight movement in a given direction in order to "read" what the pendulum is telling you.

However, as you become an expert and your swings become more pronounced, you may notice that you occasionally get a weak swing response. By this, I mean the pendulum may take a long time to respond or the swing may be short and end abruptly. If this happens, you can safely assume that the answer isn't quite as accurate as a strong swing would indicate.

For example, you ask, "Should I take the X position at ABC company?" If you get a strong, immediate and pronounced swing (either yes or no), you can be pretty certain of what your unconscious wants you to do. However, if the swing is weak, you may want to ask other questions in an effort to help clarify the response. Questions like, "Will I be happy if I stay in my current position?" "Will something better come up later on?" "Is this position a good move for my overall career?" "Is it a good move financially?" "Is this move good for my family?" This type of questioning may point out concerns and problems that have escaped your conscious mind.

A weak swing response could also suggest that you should ask the question in the future because your question or concern is not an issue at this time.

I suggest you keep a journal of your various experiments with the pendulum. You may want to divide it into different sections, dealing with different areas of questioning. The most popular areas seem to be health, finances and relationships. This is what I did when I first started working with the pendulum. In this way, I began to make sense out of what I could and could not do with the pendulum.

At first, you will find that you get the most correct answers in the areas of your life that you are already attuned to. The pendulum allows you to sharpen and make full use of the skills and knowledge you already have.

One of the most fascinating stories I came across during my research concerned a man who became a multimillionaire from playing the stock market. He said that the pendulum was the secret to his success. He was given a rather exotic-looking pendulum and was taught how to use it, but not why it worked or where the answers came from. He simply asked the pendulum whether or not he should buy a particular stock. He then bought or sold based on the responses he received from the pendulum.

This technique worked for him because he was an experienced broker; he knew the market. What happened was that if he unconsciously felt confident in a certain stock he would get a "yes." If his unconscious had doubts, he would get a "no." What did his unconscious mind know that his conscious mind didn't? Remember, the man was an experienced broker, he still did all the things a good broker should do. He studied market trends, read all the financial journals and annual reports, etc. Perhaps his unconscious would lead him toward a particular stock because an article that he read in *The*

Wall Street Journal six months ago had a bearing on this particular decision. The information in the article was no longer in his conscious memory but his unconscious, intuitive mind still had the information.

The pendulum was the tool that helped him make full use of his unconscious and conscious knowledge. As a result, he became a far more insightful person and a very wealthy man!

I gave you a logical explanation as to why the stock-broker was so successful with his pendulum work. However, some people are incredibly accurate in their dealings with the pendulum in areas that aren't so easy to explain.

For example, in every workshop that I conduct, I have a random design card chosen from one of three possibilities: a drawing of the sun, the moon or stars. This is done by a "double-blind" procedure. In other words, a third party comes to the platform and mixes the designs. He then puts one in his pocket without looking at it. No one in the room knows what the "target" card is, not even the person who selected it. I then ask the group to use their pendulums to determine the card in the man's pocket. I ask the questions, "Is the card the sun? Is the card the moon? Is the card the stars?" As I ask these questions, the participants observe the swing patterns of their pendulums. Given the odds, you would expect about one-third of the audience to get the correct card. While this does happen on rare occasions, far more often than not one-half to two-thirds of the people taking part in this little test actually hit on the correct card. I have no "logical" explanation for this.

In my opinion, based on experiences like this, when you access your intuition through the pendulum you can not only make better use of your unconscious knowledge but also get information which borders on the extrasensory. It seems magical!

Sadly, once people understand the scientific basis behind the pendulum, they oftentimes lose interest. It was fascinating when it was mysterious and magical. Now it's just a curiosity. This is a big mistake. It is also not a toy or a game. Despite the fact that you can have a lot of fun with it, the pendulum is a powerful tool which can help you gain intuitive insights in a variety of situations from which you can achieve great benefits.

You must disconnect your analytical mind from the process. During one of my workshops, a woman came to the platform. I had asked for three people who were having good success in getting their pendulums to move, and she was one of my volunteers. As I asked this small group yes and no questions, we watched their pendulums swing in answer. However, this one woman's entire body swayed in response to the questions. In other words, if the answer to the question was "no," she swayed from side to side. If the answer was "yes," she swayed forward and backward! The skeptics in the room were laughing. They were thinking, "Of course her pendulum is swinging, you can see her entire body move!" However, the skeptics missed the point. The idea of the pendulum is to bypass your conscious mind. The woman had absolutely no idea that she was moving back and forth in response to the questions. This is perhaps the clearest evidence possible that she was bypassing her conscious mind. She was so good at this that we got rid of her pendulum and just asked her questions. She unconsciously swayed to the answers and we could tell her whether she was thinking yes or no—to her total amazement. This woman was truly in touch with her unconscious mind.

It sometimes works best when it is thought to be magical. (Remember the stockbroker?) However, I feel that ethically I must explain to you exactly why this works. While I believe this is the right thing to do, I do it with some regret. Knowing too much is not always the best thing. My uncle used to say, "Too much information takes away the power of wonder."

It will take time to become proficient. Practice working with your pendulum alone for a few weeks before trying it with other people present or for the benefit of others.

It is best to explore all types of questions. "Are my car keys in the house?" "Should I ask Jackie out?" "Should I invest in stock X?" "Will my client accept this bid of Y dollars?"

A few years ago, I held a workshop at the La Costa Spa and Resort in La Jolla, California, in conjunction with a television project I was working on. The first contact any of these people had with the pendulum was at this particular workshop. Due to the nature of the program, we did follow-up interviews with the participants. The scope of the questions they asked was interesting. They ranged from stock picks to finding lost objects to career decisions.

One woman was trying to decide between two stocks. She couldn't make up her mind. She used the pendulum as a final decision-maker. The stock the pendulum indicated that she should go with gained in value and netted the woman a profit of five hundred dollars in a week's time, while the other stock remained flat.

A college student lost his car keys during a partying spree. His pendulum indicated that they were in the map pocket of the passenger door of his friend's car. They were.

A woman was trying to decide whether to leave the sunny climate of San Diego to take a government job in Salem, Oregon. The pendulum told her to go for it. She did! Two years later, I was appearing at the historic Elsinore Theater in Salem, and she came to the performance. She was delighted with her new position and new life in Oregon.

You may notice patterns of success or failure surfacing as you try different avenues of exploration with your pendulum. Some of these patterns may surprise you. You may find you have a knack for finding lost objects, matchmaking, investments or the weather! You may find that you are very successful when working the pendulum for others but not so successful when doing it for yourself or vice versa. Work on your weaknesses, and refine your strengths.

It is always important to ask clear, direct questions. Remember to ask follow-up questions if an issue needs to be more fully explored or clarified.

As your intuition begins to communicate through the movement of the pendulum, you may get answers you want to have, instead of unbiased responses from your unconscious. Establishing a healthy connection so that you receive the clearest impulses from your intuition requires disconnecting from the level of what you think you want and its subtle influence on the pendulum's movement and reconnecting to your intuitive nature and its infinite possibilities of expression.

To help facilitate that disconnection, let me give you a clearing process you may wish to utilize.

First, it is important to be in the proper frame of mind before asking the question. By this I mean, truly think the question through. Decide the clearest, most direct way to ask it. With clear intent, state to yourself: "I WANT the TRUE answer to my question." Believe it!

You will now go through a quick series of questions to double check that you are in the proper frame of mind. Aloud, ask the pendulum:

"May I have the TRUE answer?"

"Am I READY for the TRUE answer?"

If you don't receive a yes to both questions you are not in the right frame of mind. However, once you've received a yes to both questions, ask aloud the question you want an answer to.

While awaiting the answer, do so in a childlike atmosphere of innocence, expectancy and wonder. Observe the answer you receive from the pendulum.

Your final check is to ask the pendulum, "Is this the TRUE answer?" If you get a yes again, you can be certain that the answer you received came from your intuitive mind, without conscious influence.

That completes the clearing process.

One frustrating thing about working with the pendulum is the restrictive nature of yes and no types of questions. You can expand your possible answers by creating a fan-shaped chart. The chart is divided into equal sections, each containing a possible answer to your question.

Types of answers could include days of the week, specific job or career choices, months, numbers from one to whatever or, for the socially active, names of potential dates for Friday night. You could even create a fan chart with all the letters of the alphabet. The pendulum could actually spell out complete words. The possibilities are endless!

When working with a fan chart, you hold the pendulum suspended over the base or pointed end of the chart. You ask the question and then note in which direction or over which segment of the chart the pendulum swings.

There is also the possibility of conscious misuse of the pendulum. There are stories of people who demonstrated a remarkable degree of accuracy in their pendulum work. In some instances, friends and family members of the operator started to depend on the pendulum's answers. More than a few of these operators have given in to the temptation to consciously control the swing of the pendulum thereby influencing those around them to follow their way of thinking.

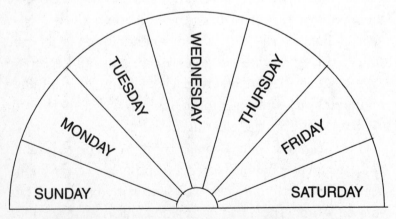

Sample fan chart showing days of the week

My uncle was a highly intuitive person and many people sought advice from him. Seeing these people depend on him for the answers to all their life questions was more than a little frightening. Ironically, my uncle only wanted to offer advice and guidance. It was his clients who turned him into an absolute authority and wouldn't do anything without his approval.

Even if you get stunning results with your pendulum, it should never be seen as a miracle or some kind of all-knowing tool of divination. You must not depend on any single decision-making tool.

The pendulum, like any intuitive tool, should be used to point out areas in your life to explore, attitudes and feelings to examine, or alternatives to consider. All of these can be very helpful in the information-gathering phases of decision-making. It shouldn't be used as a sole decision-maker, but rather in conjunction with your common sense, research and the advice you receive from others. The pendulum can help you open doors and give you important intuitive insights into your problems and in your life.

What I would like you to notice as you explore the different functions of the pendulum is that, with practice, your awareness expands. It becomes more finely tuned to an additional "sense," an additional source of knowledge—your intuition.

Good luck with your pendulum work. I can tell you that, after more than twenty-five years of working with this intuitive tool, I never cease to be amazed by it. It can really be the physical key which unlocks your intuitive abilities.

Programming Your Supercomputer

A man is what he thinks about
all day long.

Ralph Waldo Emerson

We all have the power to change our lives, to become and have whatever we want. To assist people in this process, most self-mastery programs and self-empowerment gurus advocate and incorporate affirmation techniques in their training program. The reason they do this is simple. Affirmations work! You can use them to change your life.

Affirmations are statements, positive declarations we use to reprogram ourselves—much like instructions computer programmers use to make a computer become a powerful word processor. We all need these positive programs.

Even those of us who have a naturally positive outlook.

Emile Coe, a Frenchman, was the father of affirmations. Around the beginning of the twentieth century, he became a celebrity in Europe and America by demonstrating the effectiveness of affirmations in thousands of cases. You may already be familiar with his most famous affirmation: "Every day, in every way, I'm getting better and better."

Unfortunately, many people use affirmations for a few days and when they don't get immediate results, they abandon them, believing affirmations don't work. Affirmations do work.

I began to believe in the power of affirmations in the mid-1980s. For several years, I traveled to beautiful Burlington, Vermont, each fall to do a fund-raising theater show for the United Way. After my performance one year, I met a corporate executive who was about to "throw it all away." He was going to travel the world and "find himself." During the following year, I received a few post-cards from this man. They came from exotic locations—India, the Holy Land and the like.

When I returned to Vermont a year later, he was in the audience. But he was transformed! An uptight, over-weight corporate executive was now a healthy, happy, peaceful human being. We talked for a long time after the performance. He shared his secret with me—the power of affirmations. I then told him how I would use my ana-lytical abilities to set financial goals for myself each year. I always thought it was amazing that I would come so close to meeting those goals each year, within a thousand dollars or so. When you deal with an unstructured income like mine, that's pretty good. My friend suggested that I was meeting the goals because I set them and stated them, not because of my analytical prowess. He suggested that I make my goals bigger, even if my rational abilities couldn't see where the money would come from.

The following year I set a much larger goal for myself. Guess what? I came within a thousand dollars of it! Except this time, it represented a quantum leap in income!

As you begin the process of developing affirmations, I am reminded of words that I once heard from a great teacher. He said, "That which you focus your attention on in life grows." Keep that in mind as you read this chapter.

Affirmations are really powerful mind tools that can direct your attention with laser-like precision or expand your mind to include infinite possibilities. You can use affirmations to increase your knowledge and to expand consciousness. You can use affirmations to experience greater choices, and experience greater prosperity. You can use affirmations to increase your conscious aware-ness and expand the richness of your experience.

The affirmation technique I want to teach you is a three-step process. The first step is getting clear about those things in your life that you most desire. The second step is to create affirmations that assist you in achieving or acquiring those things. The third step is to align your conscious and unconscious mind with your newly created affirmations.

Everyone begins from a different stage. For those who have never given much thought about an underlying pur-pose in life, you may want to take some time to ponder what motivates you to act. Step back and reflect on what is really important in your life, your career, your health, your personal relationships, your spiritual development and what you would like your life to become starting right now. On the other hand, some of you will create successful affirmations within an incredibly short amount of time, well grounded in your intent and purpose.

Regardless of where you begin, what is most important with this process is to create affirmations that produce intentional results. Take as long as you need, without procrastinating, to become comfortable and productive with the process. However long it takes you to complete the affirmation process, make sure you create affirmations that empower you to achieve your heart's desire. Let's begin.

Step One: Get Clear About Those Things in Life Most Important to You

Hint, the first step in creating affirmations is to suspend judgment and instead focus your intent on being open to infinite possibilities.

To assist you in the process of discovering what your possibilities are, we'll begin with three categories to inspire your thoughts: health, wealth and relationships. You may add to these categories or create new ones that represent issues that are the most important to you. Get out a blank piece of paper and create headings that include these three categories plus any others you consider important to you.

Under each of the column headings, write down the things you want more of in your life that are associated with that topic. Begin writing these things down in a manner that has meaning to you. Be as simple and clear with your wants as you can. Feel free to take as much time as you need to complete this part of the process. Your ideas will form the basis from which you will construct affirmations capable of creating greater richness in your life.

Remember to create your list using positive statements. Avoid the negative. Always frame your affirmations in the present tense and in a positive manner. Instead of saying, "I want to lose twenty pounds," you might say, "I am fit and healthy and weigh 160 pounds." Or, you would say, "I am healthy and vibrant." Not, "Hopefully, if I get lucky, I'll become healthy and vibrant."

In addition to the list of what you want to be, write down those things you want to have, like a new Mercedes or a vacation in Tahiti. This is the fun part. Putting down on paper those things you want in your life will help you to begin fashioning your affirmation.

When you write down your ideas include anything that comes to mind, regardless whether you believe you can have it or not. The idea is to expand the boundaries of your imagination. Open yourself to a world of greater possibilities. During this phase, don't worry about why you want something, or how you go about getting it, simply focus your attention on your desires—set loose your imagination.

Under the wealth category as an example you might write: "I will earn three hundred thousand dollars a year for the rest of my life." Write down everything you can think of until you feel as though you have exhausted your list of wants.

Next, it's time to begin the process of elimination. Review each item on your list, stopping at each to ask yourself why you want what you've listed. Why would I like to have three hundred thousand dollars each year?

You might answer: "Well, I would like to live in a large beachfront home in Hawaii. I would like to have a red Mercedes convertible to park in my garage next to my sailboat. And that takes money."

Continue to ask why. "Why do I want a large beach-front home?" Generally, when I get down to this layer of questioning, I begin to discover underlying motives about why I want what I want. The ones I feel most excited about are usually directly connected to an overall intent or purpose.

As an example, wanting an oceanfront home and a sailboat might reflect a deep desire to experience life to its fullest from a physical context, for example, by sailing the oceans of the world or climbing the world's highest mountains.

Next, it's time to critically examine what you've written down and decide which ideas are what you truly want. Once you've explored your entire list and have eliminated all except the most important ideas, you're ready for the final phase of step one and that is to list what you believe it would take to accomplish those things.

As an example, what would you have to do to earn three hundred thousand dollars a year?

After reflection, you might have a list that would look like this: study medicine and become a doctor; go back to college and become a CPA or an attorney; become a professional athlete; write a hit screenplay or the next Grammy-Award–winning song.

Whatever it is you have left on your list, ask yourself

what it takes from you to accomplish those things. Your affirmations will be built from your answers.

Step Two: Create Affirmations That Help You Achieve or Acquire Those Things Most Important in Your Life

Construct your affirmation based on the steps you perceive necessary to accomplish your dreams. Focus on what it takes from you to set your dreams in motion. Using the example we've been building, your affirmation might be: "Every day I make maximum use of my mental, physical and emotional abilities in pursuit of my medical degree." Or: "I grow mentally stronger and more self-assured each day as I begin my medical studies."

The following are general affirmations that you can use just as they are. However, I believe you will find the process much more effective by creating your own or incorporating the following into your own special affirmations.

I am peaceful and calm.

I feel warm and loving towards myself.

I create wealth and abundance in my life.

I always do my best with what I know.

I always use everything for my advancement.

I forgive myself unconditionally.

I give myself permission to live, love and laugh.

I live in an abundant universe.

I am my own best friend.

I am a joyful giver.

I forgive my enemies.

Step Three: Align the Conscious and Unconscious Mind with Your Newly Created Affirmations

Affirmations have their greatest effect when they align with both our conscious and our unconscious desires.

We have a unique way in which we use affirmations—one that no other program that I know of teaches. With this approach, it doesn't have to take what seems like forever before the results become obvious to you.

You've been using a pendulum to establish a connection between your conscious and unconscious intuitive self. Now you'll use the pendulum to align the affirmations you've created with your unconscious and conscious mind. Instead of the unconscious communicating with the conscious mind through the pendulum, we will reverse the process and use affirmations to program the unconscious mind for success. You see, the unconscious does not discriminate. Whatever you tell it, it will act on. By planting positive messages in the unconscious, you will get positive results. The unconscious will act in conjunction with the body to make these messages a reality in your life.

Let's start by creating an affirmation.

"I have the power to change my life and to become and have whatever I want."

That's a pretty powerful and all-encompassing affirmation.

Now, begin with the pendulum clearing process you learned earlier.

Once you are satisfied the pendulum is providing true

answers and not simply answers you want to hear, you're ready to state your affirmation.

Holding the pendulum ready for response, state your affirmation. Some people experience greater results speaking their affirmations aloud, while some find that the connection is as powerful when they state their affirmations quietly to themselves. Practice both and select the one that creates the best results for you.

As you hold the pendulum, do not try to get a response, just let it happen. When you get a "yes" swing pattern, your unconscious is lined up with your conscious desires. In the process of getting a "yes," try to notice other impressions affecting your senses. Notice the impulses that attract your attention.

If you get a "no" response, try rephrasing the affirmation. If the "no" response continues, it indicates two things. One, the old negative thoughts and feelings that your unconscious holds onto are coming back to the surface. Or, two, the goal reflected in the affirmation is something you don't really want. Either way, it is time for some introspection. You can carry out this introspection via the pendulum, asking questions of the unconscious mind.

Once you receive a "yes" from the pendulum, your mind is aligned with your desire and you should begin repeating your affirmation regularly.

Use affirmations anytime, anywhere—in line at a bank or stuck in traffic. Use your time wisely by repeating your affirmations often.

Affirmations are effective repeated silently. They are especially powerful if you repeat them to yourself as you drift off to sleep.

Affirmations are effective repeated aloud. They are especially powerful when you speak them aloud while standing in front of a mirror.

I encourage you to create and practice affirmations and to do it in conjunction with the pendulum so that you align your unconscious with your conscious mind. By doing this, I believe you will find that you have the power to change your life and to become and have whatever you want!

Just Because I'm Asleep Doesn't Mean I'm Not Working

It is in our idleness, in our dreams, that the submerged truth sometimes comes to the top.

Virginia Woolf

One-third of your life is spent asleep! It is a necessity: You can go without food for a week, but if you go without sleep for more than forty-eight hours, you will begin to hallucinate. Continued sleeplessness leads to death.

The process of falling asleep is actually a series of stages. At first, you enter the hypnagogic stage where the conscious mind begins to let go. Soft floating sensations follow, and during this stage the eyes begin to roll. This is followed by a series of jerks and spasms involving the head, arms and legs as electrical impulses are fired from the brain stem and the brain switches to a state of sleep.

As you sleep, you experience four stages. These stages range from light sleep to a fourth stage as the brain waves continue to slow. These four stages are repeated, again and again, in reverse order, as many as seven times a night.

During the fourth stage of sleep, we dream. Dreaming represents about 20 percent of our total sleep. While the first dream of the cycle may last only a few minutes, each consecutive dream gets progressively longer, often our longest dream of the night lasting more than an hour.

Although many people can't recall dreaming at all, everyone dreams. We each have five to seven dreams a night. Most of us who can recall our dreams generally only remember the last one.

When you dream, your unconscious mind truly takes over. There's an Eastern philosophy which says that your dream life is every bit as real and important as your awakened state. How often has someone asked you if you've done a certain thing or been to a certain place and you respond "sure," only to reconsider whether you actually did or only dreamt it.

The history of Western art is full of anecdotes relating dreams to creativity. Mary Shelley wrote *Frankenstein* based on dream images. Robert Lewis Stevenson based *The Strange Case of Dr. Jekyll and Mr. Hyde* on his dreams as did Bram Stoker when writing *Dracula*. Samuel Taylor Coleridge based "Kubla Khan" on a dream that he had. He wrote it down immediately upon awakening, while the work was still fresh in his mind. Richard Wagner, the German composer, wrote the opening themes of one of his most celebrated operas from dream images. Other composers, most notably, Brahms and Puccini, said their musical ideas sometimes took shape during hypnagogic states of consciousness.

One of Paul McCartney's most popular songs was the result of a dream. Upon awakening from sleep, he hurried to the piano and played the beautiful and haunting melody that enchanted him during his dream. The only thing he changed was the lyric. While it probably had great significance in his dream, he didn't think that "Scrambled Eggs" as a title and lyrical hook worked all that well, so he changed it to "Yesterday."

More recently, pop recording star Lisa Stansfield dreamed her first number one single, "Been Around the World." She awoke with the music and lyrics in her mind. She stayed up all night singing the song and then rushed to the recording studio the next morning to record it.

Julia Ward Howe wrote "John Brown's Body," and during the Civil War someone asked her why she didn't write better lyrics to the song. Howe also felt the lyrics were inadequate and she had often wanted to create new words. The day after she was questioned about the lyrics, she awoke early in the morning and the words "Mine eyes have seen the glory of the coming of the Lord . . ." came to her. She didn't push the creative process, but rather lay quietly in bed as the lyrics kept coming to her. Once she "knew" the lyrics were complete, she jumped out of bed and wrote it all down. Then, she went back to sleep, satisfied with her creative effort. Upon awakening the second time that morning, she found that she couldn't recall the lyrics at all. It was fortunate for her and for us, that she took her intuitive flash of creativity seriously or we would not have the beautiful "Battle Hymn of the Republic."

Scientific and technological insights have also surfaced through dreams and hypnagogic imagery. Niels Bohr, a Danish-American physicist, used dream images in developing atomic models. Otto Loewi, a pharmacologist, used them in analyzing nerve chemistry. Paul Ehrlich, a bacteriologist, used dream images in devising his side chain theory of molecular structure. Each of these men used dream-inspired ideas and each won a Nobel Prize for their work!

Thomas Edison was famous for taking a nap whenever he was stuck on a particular problem. He would go to sleep in his favorite chair while holding little steel ball bearings in both hands. As his mind relinquished consciousness, his hands would relax and the balls would fall into metal pans strategically placed on the floor. At the noise the balls made, Edison would jerk awake—often with an idea for solving the problem that troubled him minutes earlier. Edison's employees often commented that they didn't know how he accomplished so much as he seemed to be sleeping all the time.

The artist Salvador Dali used the same technique. Dali would lie down in bed while holding a spoon over a dish on the floor near his bed. As he fell asleep, the spoon fell from his hand, landing on the dish with the resulting noise stirring him awake. Frequently, as he awoke, he had some fascinating image in mind which he then painted.

English poet and engraver William Blake had a vivid dream one night. He dreamt that his deceased brother appeared to him and told him about a technique to produce engravings more effectively and efficiently. When he woke, he remembered the details of the dream, tested the technique and created a revolutionary new engraving process!

Dimitri Mendeleyev created the periodic table of elements. This is the same table that is found in chemistry textbooks throughout the world. Believe it or not, Mendeleyev's table came from a dream image. Not only that, but when he first created the table, he left gaps in it to account for elements which he felt existed, but had not yet been discovered. He named the properties that three of these elements would have. Over the following twenty years, each of the elements was discovered and added to the table.

I hope these stories illustrate to you the power of dreams. I want you to be excited about exploring your own dream world. You see, the unconscious can process workaday material and, in dreams, present its own solutions. Dreams can hold unexpected and welcome insights.

Many of the creative insights mentioned earlier came to these people in the hypnagogic phase of the sleep process. That drowsy stage between waking and sleeping. The body is relaxed, blood pressure drops and the heart rate and breathing slow. It's that stage when your conscious mind is giving up control to the unconscious. This happens just before going to sleep and just before waking. During these times, your chance of discovering insights revealed by your unconscious during the sleep process are at their greatest.

You can influence your dreams to help you gain insight in a certain area of your life. In other words, if you have a problem try to dream up the solution. Throughout the day and especially right before sleeping, tell yourself you want to dream about a certain subject.

Whenever possible, state the problem and ask for the solution. Put it in writing to bring it out of the abstract and into a concrete state, and then, as you relax and begin to fall asleep, keep repeating the sentence to yourself.

It's not unusual, with that intention, to find yourself snapping out of the sleep process immediately with the answer in your mind, as Edison did.

Of course, you may find yourself dreaming of the solution in the middle of the night or just upon waking as you enter the hypnagogic stage of the sleep process again.

The problem that can arise when we awaken with the answer is remembering the dream. You should keep a pad and pen by your bed, this will become your dream journal. A tape recorder can serve the same purpose. Write down or record all the details of the image you received immediately upon awakening. If a solution comes to you as you are drifting off to sleep, try to stir yourself awake and write it down or record it. Often in the moment the answer comes, it seems so clear that you feel as though you'll remember the solution forever. Unfortunately, the clarity of the moment is lost if you don't immediately write it down.

Before getting out of bed, recall any dream or image that comes to you as a result of the sleep and dream process. Write down the details as soon as possible, even if it doesn't make sense or seem to relate to your problem.

Study the images you've recorded and see if you can come up with a connection between them and your problem.

You may want to answer the following questions as you make an entry in your dream journal.

One: What image was most dominant from the dream?

Two: What activities took place in the dream?

Three: What was the strongest feeling you experienced during your dream?

Four: Can you associate those feelings, images and activities with something in your life?

Five: List any characters you remember from the dream and try to associate them with something in your life. Look for connections.

Six: Was your dream associated with a location or place? Look for connections.

Seven: Write down what you think the dream means. Briefly. Use your intuition.

Eight: What would you change about the events in your dream if you could? What does that say about you?

This brings us to our second problem area. Unfortunately, dreams are often heavily symbolic, filled with abstract images. No one knew this better than Carl Jung who was deeply involved in dream interpretation. Jung believed a message could be found in almost any dream if the dreamer took the time to analyze it carefully enough. Jung once dreamt that he was addressing large crowds instead of small classroom groups. This dream motivated him to start writing for the general public. The monumental book, *Man and His Symbols* was the result.

A good example of an abstract dream was that of Elias Howe, who invented the sewing machine. Howe spent several years on the creation of his machine, but was missing something. His rational mind couldn't find the answer. One night, Howe had an unusual dream. He dreamt he was captured by a group of savages. The tribal leader said to him that he had to finish his machine or he would be killed. In the dream, Howe was being led by the natives to his death. As he was being taken away, he noticed something unusual about the spears the natives were carrying. These spears had eye-shaped holes near their points. Howe awoke with this image in his mind. He immediately made a needle with a hole near the point instead of in the middle. This was the one detail that was missing from the successful completion of his invention. With this new needle he completed the sewing machine.

At the end of this chapter, you will find a list of some of the most common dream images and their probable meanings. However, we are such a diverse culture that meanings will differ from person to person. In other words, there are no absolutes. Feel free to use the list as a starting point to your dream analysis.

You can develop the technique of being aware of your dream as you are dreaming. It's called lucid dreaming. Being aware of your dream as you dream allows you to direct and influence what you dream. Your best results using this technique happen during the hypnagogic stage early in the morning, just before waking.

Let's say you wake up after having a pleasant, relaxing

dream. It's a dream you would like to reenter. Dr. Stephen Laberge, an expert in lucid dreaming, says that upon waking you should occupy yourself for a few minutes, with a quiet activity like reading. Then lie down and go back to sleep while concentrating on the dream you had prior to waking. Concentrate on it with the intention of entering the dream lucidly. Becoming a lucid dreamer takes practice, but can produce some extraordinary results as you learn to shift and guide your dream life.

There seems to be a connection between psychic impressions and dreams. Louisa Rhine who, along with her husband Joseph Banks Rhine, pioneered psychic research in America, gathered 100,000 cases of spontaneous ESP. Sixty-five percent of these took place while the person was dreaming.

Mark Twain dreamt of the death of his brother in a boating accident. It happened. Anne Baxter, the actress, had a dream involving the death of her famous grandfather, architect Frank Lloyd Wright. It came to pass as dreamt. One of the most famous dream premonitions concerned Abraham Lincoln who had a very real and disturbing dream about his funeral shortly before his assassination.

The first psychic experience I can recall was a result of a dream. I was nine years old. Our family was leaving to vacation at a place called Indian Lake, Ohio. The night before we left, I dreamt of arriving at the lake and being assigned a cottage. In my dream, I walked through the cottage, exploring it. The next day, when we arrived at Indian Lake, everything matched my dream. The cottage was painted blue and white just as in my dream. The floor plan of the cottage and the furnishings were exactly as dreamt, even down to an old mop propped up against the cottage on the back porch. It was this dream that captured my interest in the idea of psychic functioning.

Over the next few days, I want you to pay attention to your dreams. Have the intent to gain something from them. Practice the techniques I've outlined and see what happens. Try to dream up the solution to a problem. Have the intent to create a clear communication channel between your conscious mind and your unconscious which is roaming wild as you sleep. Use your intuition to analyze the symbolism in your dreams and see how well you do.

A proverb from the ancient Talmud says: "A dream which is not understood is like a letter which is not opened."

Dream Images We Have in Common

Falling: Something in your life requires urgent attention. Consider bringing other people in to help you with the problem. This image also connects with the idea of experiencing anxiety over the loss of control in a particular situation.

Running for your life/being chased: Usually indicates a hidden problem which you are suppressing.

Failure: There is some area of responsibility in your life which you have been avoiding.

Work: While these dreams may just recap the day's events, when coupled with the idea of failure these dreams indicate that you may feel guilty because, on some level, you do not feel you are measuring up. If you often dream this type of scenario you should work on your self-confidence.

Sex: Very popular! These don't need much interpretation. However, one thing you should be aware of is that your unconscious mind is free of the censorship of the conscious mind. Some people have sexual dreams that disturb them; they seem perverse. You should never feel this way. These are just private, unconscious fantasies.

Flying: Symbolizes overcoming a problem, breaking free of restrictions.

Naked in public: Represents the fear of being figuratively exposed in some area of your life.

Being trapped: The warning signal of an impending problem. A deadline that can't be met, etc. Can also indicate a fear of commitment.

Death: Consistent dreams of this nature could indicate real health problems. An occasional dream is probably just the result of an unpleasant reaction to some event in your life.

Violence: Frustration/anger.

Transportation: Dreams where you are in control of the mode of transportation and are proceeding on course indicate personal progress and confidence. If you dream you are a passenger and the mode of transportation is in some sort of danger, this indicates that you need to get control in a particular area of your life.

Water: This can be positive or negative, depending on the context of the dream. Still water may suggest the womb; security, bliss. Crashing waves may represent external power beyond the dreamer's control. A swimming pool could mean leisure or competition. When it appears as a large body of water with underlying mysteries, it represents the unconscious. Diving into water can suggest a search for meaning. Crossing over water signifies a transformation.

Fire: Fire can have many meanings. It can represent transformation, spiritual awakenings, love, passion and sexuality. A small, contained fire would tend to represent peace and contentment while an out-of-control blaze signifies destruction. A large fire can represent some powerful force over which the dreamer has no control.

Fish and reptiles: Fish are usually a sign of good luck unless you dream of a dead fish when the opposite is true. Alligators, snakes and the like usually represent enemies and danger.

Insects: Wasps and the like indicate threatening situations. Likewise, spiders are usually seen as threatening. Bees and ants often refer to business success through teamwork. Butterflies represent happiness and freedom.

Birds: Birds generally have good associations. Flying birds indicate independence and prosperity. Swans indicate a freedom from misfortune. A perched bird equals stability while an injured bird is a warning of some misfortune to come. A singing bird usually means happiness. Geese, ducks and the like, if making irritating noises, indicate annoying troubles. A crowing rooster represents great success and pride over something accomplished in your life.

Dogs: Traditionally they mean good luck, but a barking dog can be unlucky.

Cats: Again, good luck, unless they are attacking you and then that indicates trouble.

Rats: Rats and mice represent dangerous secrets.

Bears: Business rivals.

There are, of course, thousands of dream images. I've barely scratched the surface by commenting on only a few of the more common ones. There are many wonderful books that deal solely with dream interpretation. One of my favorites is *Dream Dictionary—A Guide to Dreams and Sleep Experiences,* by Tony Crisp. I highly recommend it.

The above can provide you with a starting point to making some sense of your dreams. However, as stated before, there are no literal interpretations that apply to everyone.

Pleasant dreams!

The Psi Factor

The philosophies of one age have become the absurdities of the next, and the foolishness of yesterday has become the wisdom of tomorrow.

Sir William Osler

This chapter explores the areas of the mind we refer to as psychic ability, the sixth sense, ESP, metaphysics or, in scientific terms, psi (pronounced like *sigh*). We will explore ideas such as mind over matter, precognition, clairvoyance and telepathy. All are exciting possibilities that lie beyond the limits of what many people currently accept as possible.

Before we go any further, let's take a look at what psi refers to. Psi is a Greek letter which references the unknown and the mind.

It is this letter which parapsychologists (scientists who study the paranormal) have chosen to represent the unknown power which causes psychic functioning. Psi functioning can be broken down into two categories. The first is extrasensory perception (ESP). Simply put, ESP means perceiving information without using your accepted five senses. ESP itself can be broken down into three components:

1. Clairvoyance: The extrasensory perception of an object or event, being aware of something that exists or existed without using your five senses, nor relying on telepathy.

2. Telepathy: Mind-to-mind communication.

3. Precognition: Seeing ahead in time, a premonition, predicting the future.

The other category of psi is psychokinesis (PK for short), the ability of the mind to influence and affect matter. Simply put, mind over matter. This aspect of psi is also referred to as telekinesis when matter is affected at a distance.

Now that we have some working definitions of just what we will be looking at in this chapter, let's get started.

The techniques you have learned so far will assist you in experimenting with the power of your unlimited mind. Some of you may feel uneasiness, have doubt or have resistance to this exploratory journey. Others will be excited, stimulated and anxious. All I ask is that you be a willing explorer. Take this opportunity to set aside skepticism and keep an open mind. You may be amazed.

You may be amused. And you may change your idea of reality.

In theory, the power of the human mind is almost limitless. In practice however, the mind is conditioned to work against itself. To expect that something can't be done. Try to recall a time in your life when a strong belief that you could not do something overcame the belief that you could. Your expectation became a self-fulfilling prophecy. You tried and you failed. What we are capable of is extraordinary. What we accomplish is often disappointing. Yet, the opposite can be true. You can also condition your mind to be, do and have whatever you want. You need only to believe. I encourage you to set aside your disbelief as we explore the extraordinary phenomena covered in this chapter.

I am reminded of a fortune-telling card with the image of a fool. It depicts a carefree character stepping out into the unknown. Eyes looking up, a foot in mid-stride, stepping toward the edge of a cliff. He has a kit bag slung on a shoulder and it contains all the things he will need on his journey. He is not tied down by old ideas and limitations. He is willing to venture into the unknown. Every great thinker, inventor, innovator or leader has been thought of as a fool at one time or another. But they chose to move ahead, taking with them all they needed in their kit sack. Intuition, determination and faith.

Now, your logical mind may tell you that exploring psychic phenomena is foolishness. But psychic phenomena is not logical; it is intuitive. Science has no known laws that govern or explain psi. Consequently, right now it is not possible to prove its existence regardless of the testing that can be done. That is how science works. So, your ideas about it are as valid as anyone's. Welcome to the new frontier!

For years science has focused its attention on the physical aspects of reality—cells, atoms, neurons, etc. Today the focus is shifting to what's between things, what connects an atom with another atom to form a molecule. What ties things together in a cohesive unit so that a group of cells can form a toe in a human body and not a finger? The search is on to discover the very fabric of consciousness—what Einstein called the "Unified Field."

An experiment, often talked about in metaphysical circles, focused on an attempt to measure what happens between cells. The test was conducted with a veteran military pilot. He was asked to view films of air-to-air combat similar to what he had experienced. As the combat images escalated and his tension mounted, test equipment recorded kinesthetic measurements of the electrical impulses his cells generated. Cell samples were taken from inside his mouth, and attached to an electrical measuring device. The cell samples were transported to a lab site five miles away. The combat scenes were run again and as the pilot began to experience stress, an amazing thing occurred. The cells transported to the remote lab site began emitting impulses which were recorded simultaneously with those recorded at the actual lab test site. When the visual stimulation stopped so did the emissions at both sites.

Something happened that can't yet be explained by conventional science, nonetheless our experience tells us that it's real, psi exists!

Some say the mind connects these cells across vast distances. Many great thinkers believe that there is a common bond, a link that connects all minds and all things. The idea of universal consciousness implies that all of humankind's thoughts and experiences are available to everyone, anytime, anywhere.

As we delve into the philosophy of contemporary science and physics, serious new questions arise about what is "real." Today, the line between reality and illusion is a lot "fuzzier." There are, in a sense, multiple realities. Accepting the possibility of something or adapting a belief, some parapsychologists believe, enables you to step outside of your preconceived perceptions and allows you to experience new phenomena that science doesn't yet know about.

There is a lot in the world we don't understand. We give them labels like the paranormal, metaphysics or extraordinary phenomena. But the truth is, on many levels, we don't really know what is going on! The trend is to want to frame things to make them understandable. People feel they have to explain things. They won't accept the fact that there are many open-ended things going on in the world today that we can't yet explain. Not knowing can be threatening to a lot of people. Most people don't want freedom. They want authoritarianism—to feel safe. Not knowing is not safe.

This desire to want to know everything breeds skepticism and cynicism. Each generation feels that they know it all. At the beginning of the twentieth century, there was a movement to shut down the U.S. Patent Office because "everything worthwhile had already been invented." The people behind the movement, driven by skepticism and cynicism, almost succeeded. Obviously, if you could go back in time and talk with these people, describing the society we live in today, they wouldn't believe a word of it.

While exploring the Great Sand Dunes National Monument, I experienced an extraordinary phenomenon of the acoustic kind. As I walked the dunes I distinctly heard a groaning sound. No one was around, and it was positively eerie! Later, I asked one of the park rangers about it. She said that the phenomenon wasn't unusual at all. It seems that if the conditions are right, dry sand will sometimes make a booming or groaning sound as you walk across it and your footsteps send sand sliding down the dunes. The interesting thing is that scientists and acoustical engineers can't explain why this is so. Remember, if science can't explain something that doesn't mean that the phenomenon itself doesn't exist.

The Great Sand Dunes National Monument is a magical place. Imagine, the tallest sand dunes in North America. Billions of grains of sand that reach heights of 750 feet and cover thirty-nine square miles. The Dunes come complete with a mysterious river that flows above ground during certain times of year and then disappears below ground during other times.

Picture these dunes and this disappearing and reappearing river. Where do you see them located? Along the ocean? In the desert? Think again! The Great Sand Dunes are in the Rocky Mountains of Colorado! What could be more magical than that?

I was appearing at a corporate event on Sanibel Island in Florida. As I met with the meeting planner, she told me of a wonderful experience she had the night before. She and a friend were swimming in the Gulf of Mexico at night. As they moved through the water, a strange trail of green light followed their movements. At first they were frightened, then they were awestruck and continued to play in the water, watching it glow green around them. They felt they were a part of an extraordinary event. When they got back to the hotel, they couldn't wait to share their experience with others. As they described this wonderful scene to a hotel employee he was very blasé about it. He then calmly explained that at certain times of year the Gulf has high amounts of phosphorous in it. As they moved through the water they stirred up the phosphorous causing the green glow which trailed their movements.

The meeting planner was disappointed that there was such a simple explanation to such an incredible event. She thought she had experienced magic. I told her that she did, in fact, experience the magical. I encouraged her to remember how she felt during the experience, the wonder, the awe. As she relived the incident in her mind a big smile appeared on her face. She said, "You know, even though I now know why it happened, it's still magic!"

Years ago, I was having lunch with two friends of two very different mindsets. One was a "new-age junkie" and loved all types of metaphysical and personal development programs. The other was a diehard skeptic. The "believer" was gushing with excitement as she had just finished her first firewalking seminar, and she had successfully walked the fire pit. The skeptic snorted. Simple physics he replied. As he started to go into a scientific explanation as to how you can walk barefoot on hot coals, my believer friend silenced him. She said, "I don't care why I can do it. I only care that I did it. I did something that I truly felt was impossible. Now, I choose to take the memory of the firewalk with me. If I did this 'impossible' thing what else can I do? Can I take off those ten extra pounds? Can I get my M.B.A.? Of course I can! I can do the impossible! I walked on fire!" I have to admit that I applauded my believer friend's attitude.

The world is full of magical, unexplainable happenings. Even when we can explain something, that doesn't make the event any less magical. Albert Einstein said there were two ways of looking at the world, as if nothing is a miracle or *everything* is a miracle! When you think about life, miracles abound! The Great Sand Dunes, the birth of a child, the fact that we exist at all! Before you say something can't be because it is just too fantastic, pause and consider the miracles that surround you every day. Don't be a gullible "believer" but accept the possibilities and rejoice in the magical world we live in.

Sometimes when we do have an explanation, it is so extraordinary that many people don't believe it (there are still those who believe that we never landed on the moon). During my stage presentation, you can often find me with my eyes taped shut with adhesive tape and five layers of cloth wrapped around my head. In this condition I am able to describe objects that people bring to stage even to the point of calling out the serial number on a piece of paper currency. While watching this, many people have got to be thinking, "It has to be a trick." But, consider the extraordinary phenomena of "blindsight." Some people who have lost their sight due to stroke or brain injury have developed this remarkable ability. Although they can't see an object placed before them, they are able to reach out and touch it or find it as if they could see it.

Psychologist Anthony Marcel of Cambridge University studied blindsight for twenty years. He found that it only occurs when the brain damage is confined to the areas of the brain which dealt with transmitting visual signals and not the neural areas that receive and interpret the signals. Although what the subject sees is no longer transmitted to the part of the brain that does the seeing, the message is still being transmitted below the level of their awareness to other portions of the brain. These parts of the brain know where the object is, allowing someone with blindsight to reach out and touch the object on the first attempt. Extraordinary! The phenomenon almost sounds supernatural in nature. Yet there is a very real, accepted scientific explanation for it.

Apollo 14 astronaut and psi researcher Edgar D. Mitchell feels that there are no supernatural phenomena, just what we know to be large gaps in what we know about natural phenomena. Mitchell and other researchers are trying to fill these gaps.

Unfortunately, modern Western thought is dominated by the fact that we have to be able to scientifically measure everything. As a result, we primarily teach in our schools only that which can be "tested" and not necessarily what we need to know to live our lives to the fullest. Students learn how to pass tests and how to please the teacher as opposed to true and deep learning which can affect lives. This philosophy carries over into the corporate world. We try to please the boss! Some of the most respected thinkers on learning, organizational behavior and excellence think that we have sold ourselves short by overemphasizing strict, narrowly defined measurement and the competition it can sometimes create.

The point? That which science can measure is limited by what it can measure and that seems pretty limiting. Don't get me wrong, I continue to be amazed at what science can do and has done. However, it is just a part of this extraordinary world that we live in and it has its limitations as well.

There are many fine arguments against the concept of psi. Often a skeptic will use the idea of Occam's razor to "debunk" what seems to be a psi experience. William of Occam was a fourteenth century logician and Franciscan friar. His idea was that when you have two competing theories which make exactly the same prediction, the one that is simpler is probably correct. A skeptic may read of an experiment wherein a psychic correctly guessed the roll of a die in each of ten consecutive tries. Someone who doesn't believe in the idea of psi functioning would say the simple answer was that the psychic cheated! To many, it is simpler to believe this, but it doesn't make it correct.

Then there are those people who see the study of parapsychology as nothing more than a huge waste of money. If there was something there it would have been proved long ago. The popular misconception is that billions of dollars are spent on parapsychological research. The reality is that there are probably less than fifty scientists in the United States and Europe who conduct this type of research on a full-time basis.

Another popular statement is that extraordinary claims require extraordinary proof. The existence of black holes, stars which have imploded and suck in all light around them, is a pretty extraordinary claim to me. There is also no way that we could prove their existence in our lifetime, yet most people accept the reality of black holes. Claims of psi functioning only sound extraordinary to those who have a limited world view.

Then there is the Sherlock Holmes argument. To paraphrase the great fictional detective, when you eliminate the impossible, the possible is the solution no matter how improbable it may seem! This assumes that we know what is possible and what is impossible. What we consider possible now is light years away from what we thought possible at the turn of the last century.

During a television interview with comedian and talk show host Dennis Miller, the subject of psychokinetic spoon bending came up. Miller, who is one of the brightest and funniest comedians I know, commented on what a worthless talent spoon bending was! If someone could bend spoons with only their minds, why couldn't they do something more practical?

While this type of question is a good example of critical thinking, my response to it is Michael Jordan! What?! Michael Jordan is arguably the greatest athlete of the twentieth century. However, he can't make his athletic talents work for him in golf or baseball (two sports he loves and has tried to excel in but has failed). The point is that Jordan's athletic prowess primarily depends on reflexes, physical conditioning and eye-to-hand coordination. If he can't make the adjustment from sport to sport, how can anyone assume to know how a "wild talent" like PK (psychokinesis) can be used when we don't even have a definite framework to explain it.

You see, we do not know enough about reality to say the laws of nature are ever violated. We just don't fully understand those laws. Nor have we sufficiently explored the innermost boundaries of perception, communication and intelligence. We cannot conclude that something impossible is happening simply because we do not comprehend all the subtle and complicated ways in which the mind processes information.

In 1903, the Wright brothers turned the mystery of flight into reality. One of the brothers publicly wondered why no one before them had discovered the secret. The key to the mystery had been waiting to be discovered since the beginning of time. Centuries before the Wright brothers, Leonardo da Vinci drew designs for airplanes. To him, the phenomenon of flight was a mystery seeking a solution. Had da Vinci discovered the secret and flown, those around him would have thought it was a supernatural event.

As great a visionary as da Vinci was, if you could travel back in time and tell him that you could point a box at the Mona Lisa and simultaneously the image of that painting would show up on a piece of glass on the other side of the planet, he probably wouldn't believe you. All I'm talking about is television.

But say Leonardo da Vinci took the skeptical and not the cynical approach. He said to you, "Okay, explain to me how this could be done." You then told him that the image travels on invisible waves, he would probably think you were nuts! Television would be a supernatural event in da Vinci's time. I don't believe in the supernatural. When someone says that something can't be because it defies the laws of science, I think what they are really saying is that there are natural laws which we do not yet understand. The field of quantum physics (the study of subatomic particles) is turning out all kinds of "unbelievable" theories right now.

There are energies which we can't see or feel. Take a dog whistle for instance. Because we can't hear it, it doesn't mean that it's not generating a sound. The phenomenon behind psi might be like the phenomenon behind television and over the next decade or next century we might be able to name the phenomenon and learn to use our minds to become aware and to generate the phenomenon at will. The fact that we can't label and control the phenomenon now doesn't mean that it doesn't exist.

Consider this: You are actually a mass of electrons, protons, neutrons and wave/particle reactions! You might be thinking, "But I'm solid." True, but at a deeper level you are energy. The body is not what it seems, but that is true of all reality. Physicists are studying things like consciousness and time reversal, phenomena previously thought to be esoteric. Concepts that seem strange to us now won't be as we understand more of their underlying physics.

William Tiller, Ph.D., is a professor emeritus of physics at Stanford and is widely recognized as one of the world's leading authorities on the structure of matter. In an interview, Tiller stated that currently we know of four types of forces: electromagnetic, gravitational, strong nuclear and weak nuclear. Tiller pointed out that two of the four forces (strong and weak nuclear) were not even suspected before the twentieth century. Tiller believes that there are other forces of nature yet to be discovered. He feels there is some type of energy operating on the physical plane which would account for psychic phenomena. Perhaps we will discover this currently unknown force in the twenty-first century!

Perhaps psi operates in its own dimension outside of, but interacting with, the four dimensions of space and time which we can perceive. Some mathematicians have suggested the universe may contain even more than four dimensions—as many as eleven or even twenty-six. Perhaps human consciousness itself belongs to one of these additional dimensions, intersecting our four-dimensional world. So, to the four "hard" coordinates of space and time we would add a fifth, "soft" coordinate of psi. If our minds could somehow tap into this extra dimension this would explain how "psychic" information travels outside of the natural laws we are presently aware of.

With the amount of information bombarding our brains, who is to say that psychic impressions aren't always there? We just ignore them, like so much else. In other words our brains are so "noisy" that we need to achieve a "quiet" mind to sort out psychic and unconscious impressions.

William James spoke of a subliminal cosmic consciousness that occasionally broke through into normal awareness. H. H. Price suggested that, from necessity, the human mind developed a mechanism to repress the continuous flow of information from the collective unconscious to prevent being flooded with the thoughts and emotions of others. During dreams and deep relaxation, the response mechanism is off guard and psychic functioning occurs.

As I've said before, the idea of a universal consciousness implies that all of man's thought and experience is available to everyone. In this view, psi effects may be explained as two or more people tuning in simultaneously to common experiences in the collective unconscious—what Jung called "synchronicity." You may have experienced this when someone you are with begins singing the same song, says the same words at the same moment or when someone finishes your sentence.

Perhaps psychic information must be meaningful to us to break through to consciousness. This is why we might be off-target investigating psi in a clinical atmosphere, guessing cards and the like. We seem more likely to have—or to recognize—psychic experiences only in emergencies, as when someone close to us is in danger of dying. The idea of a universal consciousness implies that the psychic information that your child is in danger, for example, is available to everyone, but it comes through noticeably only to you because your need to know overcomes the barriers you have built against recognizing such information. In other words, some stranger may have picked up that same information in a dream or as a random thought, but he is unlikely to recognize its meaning, or to know that it is psychic information.

Students of parapsychology have long been aware of

the fact that a large number of psychic experiences occur when emotions have been stimulated or heightened. Strong emotions surrounding fear, sickness and death have often triggered strange psychic occurrences.

Scientists have found that a single instance of overwhelming terror may alter the chemistry of the brain. They feel this may explain why some individuals are more psychic than others. The brain changes may be triggered by the terror of combat or confrontation, of childhood torture or abuse, or a one-time experience like a near-fatal auto accident. Researchers say that one in ten persons experience the disorder.

Perhaps our ability to access psychic information seems random because of our limited knowledge of how it works. It may also require belief. If consciousness determines psychic experience, maybe you can't experience what you do not believe. If psi is consciousness, what you look for is what you will find! I also believe that primitive people were much more in touch with the whole phenomenon of psi. While we may rediscover this ability in the future, I believe that it may be a form of communication that we have lost as we have become more "sophisticated." Think of it as an almost animal instinct that primitive people used to protect themselves.

In support of this theory, consider the research of anthropologist Margaret Mead. She studied a group of aborigines in Australia and concluded that they seemed to communicate telepathically all the time. For example, a mother would summon her child to her side by placing her thought "on the wind." The mother would want the child to come home and would concentrate on the child and the child would appear. The aborigines refer to this as the language of the wind or the voice of the wind; it is a common form of communication among the people.

Much of what we have covered so far concerns the mental aspects of psi. But what of PK? Can the human brain interact directly with its environment to the point that gifted people can modulate their brain waves to achieve control over events in the physical world? In the world of quantum physics, events are very bizarre. Physicist Helmut Schmidt conducted a series of tests which seem to demonstrate that psychically gifted observers can affect events at the quantum level. Schmidt built a random event generator (REG) to test for PK on a micro level. Schmidt's REG for testing PK was a sophisticated device which would register either a positive or negative "reaction" based on the random decay of a piece of radioactive material.

The reaction would consist of lights lighting in a particular pattern (clockwise or counter clockwise) based on the electron emissions of the material. Another reaction was sound. The subject would wear a set of headphones, and clicks produced by the electron emissions would register in either the subject's right or left ear. The subjects attempted to influence the random pattern of emissions by making the lights go in a clockwise direction or the clicks sound more frequently in the right ear.

With such a random and uncontrollable event (the decay of a piece of radioactive material), you would expect a totally random pattern. However, according to Schmidt, all of his subjects were able to influence the pattern to a degree that was slightly better than chance. Schmidt also had one subject who was so good that her results were a billion to one against pure chance.

The point is, if (as Schmidt's experiments seemingly demonstrated) human minds can influence the micro world, why not the macro world as well? Micro particles behave in an odd fashion, tunneling through barriers and showing up in places that classical physics insists they should not be. All objects are made up on innumerable micro particles. If these tiny units can pass through barriers, might it not be possible, under certain conditions, for an entire object to pass from one side of a wall to another?

Think of this: if you place a piece of cardboard over the mouth of a drinking glass and then sit an ice cube on top of the cardboard and place the entire affair out in the sun, the ice cube would melt, absorb into and through the cardboard, and drip into the glass where it could be refrozen back into its original form. Matter through matter!

A basic law of physics dictates that no object can be moved without an expenditure of energy. If a table is levitated, for example, some force must cause it to rise. But where would the energy come from? And how could a person tap into this energy and direct it? Heat or sound might supply the necessary force. Sound or heat waves might coalesce into a form of coherent energy which could then be directed at an object. This would be similar to how a laser beam acquires its power, by concentrating and directing light. Perhaps specially gifted people can use their will or consciousness to seize energy and consolidate it into a force that is capable of moving objects.

According to one researcher, cooling a room by one-degree Celsius would release enough energy to lift an armchair several hundred feet in the air. Another psi researcher maintained that everyone present when a table seemed to levitate had lost a few ounces of weight. This might indicate that all of those in the group had somehow contributed a small amount of their own energy to the apparent PK.

Now that we have developed a framework for psi, I hope your appetite is whetted, and you are ready to try to develop your own psi abilities. A number of exercises follow which cover all areas of psychic functioning. Try everything! You may find yourself drawn to one or more of the "tests." You may enjoy working within one realm of psi more than another. You may find that you "star" in one area and get mediocre results in others. You will never know your personal psi-quotient until you try all the tests. Some of them may sound silly to you. A lot of this has to do with the way you naturally process information. For example, my wife is a very "touchy-feely" person. She loves the concept of psychometry and is very good at it. I am a very visual person and enjoy scrying. She feels scrying is silly; I am not particularly adept at psychometry.

While I don't think it is absolutely essential that you believe in psychic functioning, I do believe that you will progress much faster if you do. When you begin practicing these exercises have the intention to suspend your critical disbelief. If you do you will be amazed at the results.

I am betting that you will have some experiences that will cause you to believe in things you may seriously question now. We tend to accept or reject ideas based on personal experience. My father is one of the most rational and analytical men I know. Years ago he experienced the extraordinary phenomenon of astral projection. He was in hospital for a gallstone operation. At one point he was "out cold" when two nurses came into his room. They were standing next to his bed, and my father said he was watching them from behind and above, from a corner of the room. He could see the backs of the nurses, and he could see himself in bed. I questioned him, "Are you sure you were not just half-awake and heard them talking and visualized the whole scene in your imagination?" He responded that he knew this wasn't the case. He said he couldn't explain it, but he just knew that it was his consciousness, soul or whatever in the corner of the room looking at his body! I was more excited about it than he was.

I have tried to experience astral projection or have an out-of-body experience for years and have not been able to. My skeptic father has one and thinks it's no big deal! The point is that had you asked my father prior to this experience if astral projection was possible, he would probably have laughed at you! Once he experienced it, he took it for granted. To him astral projection is now a fact of life.

Relaxation and meditation are the best possible preparation for using your psi abilities. Be physically relaxed yet passively alert. If you are too aggressive or approach the task with a do-or-die attitude, you are likely to fail. Most people, when they start to get extrasensory information, dismiss it simply as being their imagination. As soon as they consciously think this, the energy flow ceases. Don't try to analyze what comes through to you. Simply remain relaxed and receive it passively. There is plenty of time to evaluate your experience later. Don't get hung up on why this works. This isn't really a scientific validation of psi. It is a course of action to better your life, to make you more powerful. Science doesn't fully understand electricity or magnetism, yet we make use of these things daily. In other words, I don't understand electricity, but I can turn on a light switch and light up a room. If it works, it works. Don't spend your time questioning it, spend your time learning how to use it.

As you try these exercises, intend to notice the difference between a true ESP flash and a guess. Try to cultivate that feeling as you go through the various exercises. And don't be impatient. Think of the following tests as exercise equipment for your mind. It takes time to look like Arnold Schwarzenegger. It will probably take time for you to learn to freely tap into your psi abilities.

Let's begin!

Three Emotions

Get together with someone you feel comfortable with. Face each other either sitting or standing. Sitting comfortably is preferred. One person closes his or her eyes and thinks about a past experience either happy, sad or neutral. The other person tries to pick up on the emotion. Statistically speaking, you should be correct one third of the time. For example, nine attempts should result in three successes. Four or more successes in nine attempts go beyond mathematical odds and indicates that something unusual is happening. The interesting thing about this experiment is that as you try it, not only will you become more proficient with picking up the emotion being thought of, but you may find yourself picking up details of the actual event the person is thinking of!

Scrying

The image of a turbaned fortune-teller peering into a crystal ball is legendary. There is such a thing as crystal gazing, and you can learn to cultivate that talent. The technical term for it is scrying.

The "magic," so to speak, is not in the crystal ball. The crystal merely acts as a focus for the impressions of the inner mind to develop. The idea is to use the ball as a focusing device to help the conscious mind touch the unconscious. You don't need a crystal ball in order to scry. You can peer into a glass of water or a mirror. For example, I use a darkened leaded glass mirror made specifically for scrying.

Before attempting to scry, go through one of the visualization exercises presented earlier in this book in order to focus and calm your mind.

As you complete the visualization open your eyes and look into your scrying device of choice (glass of water, mirror, crystal ball, etc.). Relax and gaze steadily into the scrying surface. Breathe rhythmically and keep your mind from wandering. Concentrate all your attention at the scrying surface. Don't try to see anything specific. Just intend to be receptive to any images. At first, you may see a dark cloudiness. After this, you will begin to see vague images in the object. Allow the images to develop. Literal images tend to appear on the left side of the scrying surface while the more abstract images appear on the right side. If the meanings of the images aren't clear to you, allow yourself some time to think over what you saw. In many ways, this is very similar to analyzing dreams.

If you have a particular problem you want a solution to, ask the question aloud. Go through the meditation or visualization and then look to the scrying surface. The images that appear should have a direct bearing on the answer to your question.

Don't be discouraged if you don't get results with this at first. It is a very difficult technique to master. Even experienced scryers can take up to fifteen minutes before any images develop.

Automatic Writing

The most elaborate form of unconscious communication is automatic writing. Automatic writing is the act of writing directed by the unconscious with no conscious thought involved.

No less than Tennyson and Yeats experimented with automatic writing to create prose.

In 1907, a man by the name of Frederick Bligh Bond was in charge of the excavation of Glastonbury Abbey. Bond tried the automatic writing process and got a number of messages in both Latin and Middle English. These messages detailed the location of a medieval chapel below the Abbey's ruins. As the excavation continued Bond's messages proved accurate.

A modern example of automatic writing may be facilitated communication. This is a technique used to "communicate" with autistic children. The facilitator holds onto the child's wrist as the child, in theory, types out messages on a keyboard. Remarkable communication has been reported using this technique. The child and facilitator have created poetry and written long, verbose messages. Unfortunately, when someone not emotionally involved with the child or the idea of facilitated communication— in other words a true, disinterested third party—acts as the facilitator, communication seems to cease. This indicates that, on an unconscious level, facilitators who successfully receive communication might actually create it themselves through automatic writing. There is a very strong possibility that the messages are coming directly from the facilitator's mind and not the child's.

Facilitated communication sets up the perfect conditions for unconscious communication: a true desire to communicate and the belief that the facilitator is not directing the typing on the keyboard. These two important factors provide the conscious disconnection needed for unconscious communication to take place. Many of the facilitators can't believe that they are doing the typing because they are creating poems and writing in ways that they feel they couldn't create. I think this indicates the creativity that lies in everyone's unconscious.

However, we must not discount the notion that facilitated communication can be real communication between two people. While automatic writing appears to be a reasonable explanation, it could also be that in certain cases, when you have two emotionally connected people involved in the process, some type of mind to mind communication is taking place.

The process of automatic writing is easy to explain but difficult to master.

Step One: Put your pen to paper. From this point on, pay no conscious attention to the pen or paper.

Step Two: Go through a meditation/visualization.

Step Three: Open your eyes but look out the window, at the wall, or the flame of a candle. (You can also choose to keep your eyes closed.)

At this point, you will start to write or at least scribble on the paper. At first it will be hard to read. But, the more you work with it, the easier it will become to decipher. Going back to our first pendulum exercises, you may want to start by asking simple questions you know the answer to (for example, "How old am I?") This is just to get familiar with the technique.

Once you get proficient, you can expand to any and all areas—problems with your life, questions about the future. Let yourself go with a creative stream of consciousness through automatic writing. Entire books have been written using automatic writing. You may even write the great American novel!

You don't have to use pen and paper. Many people work with typewriters. Personal computers, with the sensitivity of their keyboards and the speed with which they work, are also ideal tools for developing automatic writing. Experiment with different mediums and work with the one you get the best results with or feel most comfortable with.

Psychometry

Psychometry is a form of clairvoyance. It involves holding an object and picking up impressions concerning the object itself or its owner. The idea is that our personality "rubs off" on our personal possessions and by holding an object we can sometimes sense the owner's personality as well as a bit about that person's past, present and future.

Step One: Begin using items that have been worn or carried by someone for at least a year. Avoid antiques initially, since their list of owners is typically long. Consequently, the vibrations you perceive may be those of a former owner now long dead. You can work with items made of anything, but to begin with avoid objects made of cloth, paper or wood because they are hard to read. The best items to begin with are small items made of precious material such as gold or silver.

Step Two: Get settled using the relaxation exercises we addressed earlier. Breathe slowly and deeply, following the relaxation exercise for thirty seconds before touching the object.

Step Three: Pick up the item. How you hold it is up to you. Some prefer to hold it cupped in both hands. Others prefer holding it in one hand while stroking or touching it with the other hand. If you decide to hold it in one hand, determine which hand feels the most natural or comfortable holding the object. Use that same hand every time you psychometrize. Hold the object lightly. If you squeeze it, you may lose the vibrations. It may be helpful to close your eyes.

Step Four: Become aware of the shape, texture and feel of the item. These are all physical properties of the item. Gradually you will feel the time is right. Allow yourself to extend these perceptions. Mental images will come to you. No need to try too hard. In fact, trying will have the opposite affect of the one you want. Stay relaxed and let it happen.

Step Five: Take a deep breath and then give voice to the images and feelings which come to you. Just "talk off the top of your head." Don't worry about what you are saying. If you become concerned about being correct, your conscious mind will take over and you'll lose the feelings. Simply say whatever comes to you.

Step Six: If the owner of the item is present ask him or her how correct you were. If the owner asks questions, respond with the first thing that comes into your head. If the owner is not present, write down all of your impressions or, best of all, have someone else write them down while you're talking, or record the session.

When you first begin, you will tend to pick up the most emotional part of an object's history. Consequently, you'll have a tendency to pick up feelings of illness, emotional problems, accidents and so on. Don't let this disturb you. It's a sign that you are making good progress. You will start to pick up the more positive feelings in time. Most psychometrists find it easier to pick up the more negative energies rather than the positive ones. It does not mean that the person you are reading for is a bad person. It's just that the more emotional it is, the greater likelihood of it coming through. You may experience a great deal of happiness if the object is associated with a celebration such as a wedding or birthday.

You can use a photograph to gather impressions. Pay attention to the clothes the people in the photograph are wearing. Pay attention to the detail in the background. This will give you a few first impressions. Then hold the photograph in one hand, or lay it face up on a table, and gently pass the other hand over the photograph. Some people like this hand to actually touch the photograph, but most prefer to have their hand pass just above. After a few passes, impressions will come into your consciousness. Say them aloud and have them recorded.

Some people have amazing success with psychometry the very first time they try it. I hope you're one of those people.

Clairvoyance

The following tests are variations on the theme of clairvoyance.

Test One: Find a small wooden box that can be locked, or a bag that can hide its contents. Ask a friend to ask someone else to place an object inside the box. This is to insure that neither your friend nor you know what has been placed inside. When the box is returned to you, relax completely and move your hands around the box, a few inches from its surface. Remain as relaxed as possible and allow as much time as is necessary. You may feel a tingling sensation in your fingertips, and that is a good sign. Try to describe what you "feel" is inside the box. If you don't receive impressions after ten or fifteen minutes, simply put the box away and try again the next day. It's best to do this at a time when you feel refreshed. When trying again, take hold of the box. It will make the test easier. This is not an easy test. Yet it is one that is well worth persevering with.

Test Two: Whenever you visit somewhere for the first time, visualize what is inside the cupboards and drawers of the room you're in. Do this often. You will surprise yourself about how accurate you become with regular practice.

Test Three: You have an appointment with someone you've previously not met. You've never been inside this person's office or home. The night before the appointment, relax and visualize the office or home where you'll be visiting the next day. See the distinctions of the different rooms. Pay attention to details. Look at magazine covers, furniture styles and colors and any specific, identifying information. When you keep the appointment, you'll be able to verify your success. (When trying this test, also imagine how you want the situation to turn out and positively project that outcome into your visualization.)

Test Four: Using the same model as above, change the intent slightly to focus on the person you will be meeting with. What will he or she look like? What will the person be wearing?

Test Five: Try listening to your clairvoyant abilities the next time the phone rings. Before you answer it, see if you can determine who is at the other end.

The last few tests had you use clairvoyance in your everyday life. You should strive to come up with unique ways to get psi to function in your everyday life. For example, my wife and I are always getting separated in shopping malls and at antique flea markets. As you probably know, this can be frustrating. Instead of becoming irritated, I use it as an excuse to exercise my psi ability. I try to sense where my wife is before running around and trying to find her.

It is now time to turn our attention to PK. I really feel that psychokinesis is the most difficult of all the psi abilities to harness. I also believe that the extraordinary phenomenon of ideomotor response covered in The Intuitive Pendulum chapter of this book is the key to unlocking the door to your PK abilities. For this reason, you will find several exercises in the Mind Games chapter which not only demonstrate ideomotor response and the mind body connection, but which also may lead to PK. I'll also teach you how to bend spoons!

Mind Games

Man's mind, stretched to a new
idea, never goes back to its
original dimension.

Oliver Wendell Holmes

Hopefully, I have given you a lot to think
about in this book. We've explored
some extraordinary concepts. You have been
given step-by-step instructions on how to
develop various fascinating aspects of your
mind. Now, it's time to have some fun!
Welcome to mind games!

This chapter consists of a series of exercises, primarily designed as games, that will
help you test and enhance your ESP and intuitive capabilities. Some of the exercises will
deal with psychology, others with intuition

and the unconscious, and we will revisit the mind-body connection. Then there will be those exercises which will yield surprising results that are not as easy to explain. Hopefully through trying these exercises you will touch on the areas of psi functioning that we covered in the previous chapter. And don't forget your pendulum! The games are best played with groups of friends although many of the tests can be done by one or two people. Game playing is perfectly suited as a way to test ESP. I think intuition and even psychic ability play a part in many traditional games. If you don't believe me, talk to any serious poker player.

In order for you to get the most out of this chapter, I encourage you to approach these exercises in a light-hearted way, have fun with them. Believe in the possibility that there is more to our minds than we are accustomed to. When you try an exercise, want it to succeed, believe that you can do it. This attitude coupled with the fun and excitement of "playing" these "games" with your friends and associates will greatly increase your chances for success. Best of luck to you, I "predict" you'll be amazed at some of the results you will receive!

It's All in the Cards

The following tests will duplicate the ESP laboratory experiments made famous by Dr. Joseph Banks Rhine at Duke University. I debated whether to start this chapter with these experiments. They are interesting, but the tests are very clinical. You'll need to run through over one hundred guesses before your results can be considered

statistically significant. In short, it gets boring! You begin
to lose your edge, your interest. The emotional tie is no
longer there and your scores will suffer. However, the
tests provide a perfect introduction to ESP, so that is why
we are starting here.

First, a little history. Dr. Joseph Banks Rhine started an
ESP testing laboratory at Duke University in 1930. Rhine
continued his work at Duke until his retirement in 1965.
At that time, he created the independent Foundation for
Research on the Nature of Man to carry on his research.
The Foundation is still operating today as the Rhine
Research Center.

Rhine's early research focused on ESP testing cards.
The pack consisted of five different symbols (circle, cross,
wavy lines, square and star) repeated five times each for
a total of twenty-five cards in the pack. With these cards
the primary components of ESP can be tested:

Clairvoyance: The extrasensory perception of an
object or event, being aware of something that exists or
existed without using your five senses, nor relying on
telepathy.

Telepathy: Mind-to-mind communication.

Precognition: Seeing ahead in time, a premonition,
predicting the future.

You don't need an authentic pack of ESP testing cards
to duplicate the Duke experiments. All you have to do is
get a regular pack of playing cards. We'll go over the
basic test procedures for each of the three categories of
ESP described above. Then I'll tell you about some of the

startling results Rhine obtained at Duke, and then I'll give you some tips for handling the cards.

In the following descriptions, you will be guessing either the suit of the card (heart, spade, diamond or club) or the color of the card, simply red or black. I suggest you try it both ways as you may find yourself more "in tune" to one or the other.

Testing for clairvoyance: The pack is thoroughly shuffled and then cut. You then guess down through the pack as to which card (suit or color) is on top, second and so forth through the fifty-two cards. You record your impressions on a pad, and the cards are not looked at until after you make all fifty-two guesses.

Testing for telepathy: Two people are needed for this. One person, the sender, shuffles and cuts the pack. The sender then looks at the top card and concentrates on it. The other subject, the receiver, then guesses as to the card's identity (suit or color only). Once the receiver records his impression, he notifies the sender who then turns up the second card and so on through the complete run of fifty-two cards. None of the guesses are verified until after all fifty-two cards are "guessed."

Testing for precognition: The pack remains in its case. You write down fifty-two "guesses" as to either suit or color (depending on which system you choose to use) on a sheet of paper. The pack is then removed from the case, shuffled and cut. The new order is now verified and compared against your guesses.

How do you know if anything extraordinary happened? Compare your results to the following table. It works this

Success in Card Tests Using Suits

Number of Runs	Chance	Fair	Good	Outstanding
1	13	15	18	21
4	52	58	65	72
10	130	146	163	179
50	650	687	725	762
100	1300	1352	1404	1456

Success in Card Tests Using Color

Number of Runs	Chance	Fair	Good	Outstanding
1	26	31	36	42
4	104	117	133	143
10	260	294	328	359
50	1300	1375	1450	1524
100	2600	2704	2808	2912

way: The "Number of Runs" column heading relates to the number of complete cycles through all fifty-two cards. Let's say that over a period of five days, you completed ten complete cycles of cards, attempting to guess suits. When you add up all of your correct "hits," you intuited 166 correctly. Since you surpass the minimum of 163 correct "hits," you qualify in the "Good Success" category.

As you can tell by the tables, you need to guess at a lot of cards! You don't have to "hit" that often, but it gets monotonous and repetitious. You should only use one method of testing (either color or suit) when tabulating your results and test for only one area of ESP at a time.

The tests can, and should, be carried out over a long period of time (once a day for a week or even a month, for example). The idea is to keep the procedure fresh. Most people find that the second or third run is their best. By that time, the subject is familiar with the cards and the testing procedure(s), but the novelty is still there. As a rule, the longer the testing goes on, the more the scores decline.

As an example, Rhine tested a man named A. J. Linzmayer at Duke. On his first run, Linzmayer called the first nine cards of the pack correctly against odds of about two million to one! The next day, the same thing happened. Linzmayer was tested over a period of time and his scores began to decline, but his overall hits for 300 calls were 119, more than double chance.

Perhaps Rhine's most outstanding subject was a young divinity student named Hubert Pearce. Pearce averaged ten hits out of twenty-five cards on his first five thousand calls. Pearce seldom made a long string of hits as did Linzmayer. The exception was when Rhine began to bet Pearce one hundred dollars for every hit. The bet seemed to spur Pearce on; it added excitement and Pearce won twenty-five hundred dollars by hitting every card in a run of twenty-five. Rhine called this the most phenomenal thing he had ever seen. The odds against this happening are 298,023,223,876,953,125 to 1!

While Pearce had incredible success over a long period of tests, there were times he did poorly or operated at just chance levels. These were times when he was bored or depressed. Most notably his scores declined considerably after his fiancé left him.

In response to criticism by psychologists, an elaborately controlled series of ESP tests was conducted in 1939 at Duke. It was probably the most completely controlled experiment ever carried out in a psychology laboratory. The end result of these tests showed significant evidence of ESP even though the procedure was burdened with complicated precautions.

With outstanding subjects like Pearce and Linzmayer and with further documentation from other subjects on a statistically significant scale (if not the overwhelming success of Pearce and Linzmayer), Rhine and his associates felt that ESP was proven. Rhine's research success was also duplicated by many parapsychologists (scientists who study psychic phenomena) around the world.

You and your friends can run your own tests. Entire groups of people can participate at once using the tests described earlier. It's fun for a while and who knows, maybe you'll find another Pearce among your acquaintances!

I'd like to make some suggestions. Just "play" with the cards on your own and see what happens. While you're watching television, shuffle and mix the cards. Every once in a while quickly turn your attention to the pack and just make a guess. Listen to your intuition, follow your hunches. Watch some more TV and then suddenly go back to the pack and name a suit or color off the top of your head. Using this relaxed procedure, I predict you'll be surprised by some of the results you'll get.

I would like to give you a few more exercises dealing with playing cards. These will also help you get in touch with your extrasensory self and, in keeping with the theory behind this chapter, they will help break the monotony of the more structured tests described previously.

Remove all of the cards of one color or suit from the pack of cards except for one card of that color/suit (this will be your target card). Spread the remaining cards face down on a large table. Try to sense which is the target card by holding your hand a few inches over the cards. This is a technique you can include others in. Who can find the target card in the least number of tries?

Take five of the same color card (let's say red) and add a sixth black card. Mix these face down on a table. Hold your hand over each card until you sense which card is the odd one. Check the card to see if indeed it is the odd card. Statistically speaking, if you "hit" more than four times in twenty tries you are scoring above mathematical odds.

Pick your "favorite" card. By this I mean choose a card you are drawn to. It might be the queen of hearts or the ace of spades. Perhaps you have a favorite number, three, and you like a particular suit, diamonds, so the three of diamonds will be your favorite card. Thoroughly mix the pack of playing cards. Now deal them, one at a time, in alternating piles, into two equal piles. Try to intuit in which pile your target card rests. Look through that pile. If you were correct, wonderful! Mix that pile (discarding the other pile) and deal the cards into two equal piles again. Try to intuit in which pile your target card rests. Keep this up until you miss or until you get down to just your target card. Statistically speaking, you should be correct 50 percent of the time. If you hit above 50 percent you're doing something right!

As we have discussed, intuition happens in a flash. It could communicate with you as a subtle impulse, or in full Technicolor. So the point is, don't think about it, just go with your first impression or impulse.

While you are trying these various tests, I want you to notice how you are feeling. Begin to notice the distinction between an obvious guess and an intuitive knowing. Don't force it, just have the intention to notice the distinction.

Psychometry

We covered psychometry in a previous chapter, but I want to give you a fun psychometry test involving a group of people.

Each person is asked to bring with them a personal object, the more personal the better. It should be an object that is not immediately identifiable as belonging to a woman or a man. Each person is given an envelope and told to secretly place their object inside. The envelopes are mixed and one is selected. One of the group holds on to the object and begins to "psychometrize" it. How do you do that? You just start talking off the top of your head while holding the object. Be aware of the object, its texture, etc. Close your eyes, clear your mind and just start talking. Say whatever comes to mind. Don't let logic enter into this—go with your feelings. Talk about the personality of the object's owner, describe what you feel concerning the owner's past and present, make projections as to the owner's future.

Once you've finished, have the owner identify himself or herself and either confirm or deny your impressions. The remaining envelopes can then be passed on for someone else to try.

An abbreviated version of this is to hold onto the object and to try and sense if its owner is male or female.

Remote Viewing

Remote viewing began in the 1970s and is still a hot subject in parapsychology (the study of psychic phenomena) circles today. Technically speaking, remote viewing is the acquisition and description by mental means of information blocked from ordinary perception by distance, shielding or time. A popular remote viewing test involves two participants, a sender and a receiver. The receiver stays in the laboratory while the sender leaves the lab and arrives at a randomly selected location. The sender then walks around and observes their surroundings, trying to send the information telepathically to the receiver. The receiver attempts to pick up the information, seeing through the eyes of the sender as it were. Using this testing procedure, parapsychologists have recorded some amazing hits.

What we are going to attempt here is not really remote viewing, but it will simulate it.

For this test you will need ten or more photographs or postcards. The images should be as different as possible. The photos or cards are thoroughly mixed. From this point the test can be carried out in one of two ways.

The first way is to have one person designated as the sender with the rest of the group acting as receivers. The sender randomly selects a card and studies it, trying to send the image to the entire group. Each member of the group records their impressions (examples, indoor or outdoor scene, presence of water, people in the image, etc.) Everyone should be encouraged to go with their first impressions. When everyone has had time to record their impressions the image is revealed. See how close each person came.

The second way to attempt this test is to have a post-card or photo blindly selected. In other words, no one knows its identity. The card is placed in an envelope and guesses are made by the entire group. This is known in parapsychology as a "double-blind" experiment.

The first procedure is designed to test telepathy while the second tests clairvoyance.

An interesting way to carry out this test is to have everyone speak aloud of their impressions. Take note of the similarities that keep cropping up and compare those similarities to the actual target image. As with the psychometry exercise before this, it is hard to evaluate success with this test on a statistical level. However, successes and failures will be obvious.

Swaying

This "stunt" and the one that follows are both old parlor games. They are completely unrelated as to why they happen, but they're fun and both involve a group of five people.

One person is elected to be the receiver. This person goes into another room while the rest of the group decides on a direction—either forward, backward, to the right or to the left. Once a direction has been decided upon the receiver comes back into the room.

Four people form a circle around the receiver. One person in front, one in back, one on the left side and one on the receiver's right side. The receiver stands straight up, head facing forward, feet together.

At this point, each of the four people put their hands on the receiver's shoulders. The receiver is instructed to close his or her eyes as the circle members concentrate on the direction in which they want the receiver to sway. The receiver should have no fear of falling as they are being supported by the circle members.

The circle members must now concentrate and focus all their attention on the direction in which they want the receiver to sway. Project the direction to the receiver by thought, visualize the person swaying in that direction, will them to do so.

The receiver must relax, clear his or her mind and follow any urge to fall in a particular direction without resisting. When the receiver does sway take note of the direction and then support the person so he or she doesn't fall.

Try the test at least four times, alternating receivers if you want. If the receiver sways in the correct direction one out of four times, that's chance. More than that indicates that "something" is taking place.

Levitation

I'm sure you've done this before. But do it again! It's fun and the phenomenon is truly interesting to observe. Perhaps it is an example of teamwork, focused energy or mind over matter!

Again, we need five people. A person of average height

and weight is chosen to sit in a chair. Four other people position themselves around the seated "subject." Each person clasps his or her hands together, extending the index fingers. Two people place their index fingers under the subject's knees. The other two place their index fingers under the subject's arms, near the subject's armpits. At this point the four try to lift the person into the air using just their index fingers. You probably won't get the subject out of their seat and, if you do, it won't be easy.

Now that you know how difficult it is to lift the subject in this manner, you're going to try again—but this time with a little help from positive visualization.

All five people must close their eyes and breathe in unison as they count from one to ten. The subject must imagine that he or she is becoming incredibly light, as light as a feather. The "lifters" must imagine themselves becoming incredibly strong.

When the group reaches the count of ten, the lifters open their eyes and reposition their hands underneath the subjects knees and armpits. The lifters then count to three aloud and at the count of three they try to lift the subject. If done correctly, you'll find the subject virtually "flying" into the air with no strain at all on the part of the lifters.

Spoon Bending

Perhaps the most controversial area of parapsychological research is psychokinesis (PK for short), the ability of the mind to alter and influence solid matter.

Perhaps the most controversial figure in parapsychology is the Israeli psychic and PK superstar, Uri Geller.

During the 1970s, Geller created a worldwide sensation. He claimed he could bend metal through the power of his mind. He was tested in laboratories around the world, under very strict conditions and he passed many of those tests, causing more than a few reputable scientists to judge his abilities as real. Magicians yelled "fraud" and a few of them were able to duplicate much of what Geller did both in and out of the lab. (I think it might be important to point out that on three occasions Geller was tested by magicians and on all three occasions the magicians could not explain what he did, choosing to believe that something other than conjuring was taking place.)

The debate still goes on today. Is Geller for real or just a clever trickster? I'm not going to debate that question one way or the other. However, if you're a skeptic you might change your mind after you try the following exercise.

Get a spoon, a typical teaspoon. Not something so strong that you need a vise to bend it and not one that a strong gust of wind would put a crease in. Something in between—your average kitchen teaspoon. You can do this on your own, but it's more effective and fun to do this in a group with everyone taking part, each person working with his or her own spoon.

Everyone holds his or her spoon in the same manner. Hold the bowl of the spoon in one hand and the end of the spoon's handle in the other hand. Test the spoon first. Don't bend it out of shape but get an idea of the amount of pressure needed to put a bend in it.

Now all the participants close their eyes and begin to count slowly from one to twenty, breathing in unison as they count. Breathing in and out on each count. As the group is counting, everyone is to imagine that their spoon is becoming soft and pliable, like melting plastic or taffy. Believe it is happening and will it to happen. Really focus and concentrate, "feel" the spoon becoming soft. (It would probably help in this demonstration, indeed, in all of these exercises, to play some upbeat, "new age" instrumental music to set the mood.)

If all has gone well, when you reach twenty the spoon will feel like rubber and will remain that way for a few seconds. With your eyes still closed, physically bend the spoon, twist it around, it will be like putty in your hands. Really go to work on it!

After a few seconds you will feel the spoon start to "cool." You will start to feel more resistance. At this moment stop physically manipulating the spoon, open your eyes and take a look. The condition of your spoon may really shock you!

You will find a very interesting account of spoon bending in Michael Crichton's book, *Travels*. Crichton talks of taking part in a spoon-bending party wherein the participants followed similar procedures to those outlined above. Crichton successfully bent his spoon. He knew there wasn't a trick to it, and he was in a room full of people who got the same result. The interesting thing is that Crichton took all of this in stride saying, "At first the event appears exciting and mysterious, but very quickly it becomes so mundane that it can no longer hold your interest. This seems to me to confirm the idea that so-called psychic or paranormal phenomena are misnamed. There's nothing abnormal about them. On the contrary, they're utterly normal. We've just forgotten we can do them."

Table Tilting

For years I've performed an effect in which a thoroughly examined table moves about the stage while my fingertips and those of an audience volunteer lightly touch the table's top. The table eventually lifts off the stage and is suspended, at my fingertips, over the heads of the spectators in the front row! This has been one of the most talked about features of my live presentation. In fact, it was this very demonstration which resulted in my first appearance on *The Tonight Show with Jay Leno,* where I had the honor of performing the demonstration with both Jay and Eddie Murphy. What a night that was! And now I'm going to tell you how to simulate this strange effect.

Table tilting is at least one hundred years old. At the turn of the century, it became a favorite pastime of people throughout the world. It was actually the forerunner of the famous Ouija board.

For this exercise, you will need a small, lightweight but sturdy table with four legs. Set the table on a flooring surface that will allow the table to move about. For example, tile, hardwood or linoleum would be fine. Don't do this on a carpeted floor. Position four people around the table, one on each side. All four people need to place both hands flat on the table's top. The little finger of each hand should lightly touch the little finger of the hand of the person on either side of you.

Start breathing in unison, counting aloud from one to five and then will that table to move. Imagine it tilting from side to side. Really concentrate on it. It may take some time, but don't give up on it. Keep with it. You may just feel movement at first, then it may begin to tilt and eventually "walk" around the room!

Some people get the table to tap out answers to questions. The table will tilt to one side and then rest. Two tilts or "taps" will signify "no" while one tap will mean "yes." You can try this, but you've already found a much easier and more effective way of doing this in The Intuitive Pendulum chapter of this book.

So, what causes the table to move? Well, it's not spirits, as people at the turn of the century thought, and it's not PK, but it is, of course, our old friend ideomotor response. Your unconscious minds control the movement of the table. Your concentration causes your unconscious to send signals to your body which causes the table to move. The unconscious thought creates a physical reaction. For a full description of this extraordinary phenomenon please refer to The Intuitive Pendulum chapter of this book—see, I told you not to skip it!

One more thing. I strongly suggest that you videotape your table-tilting efforts. One day you may find all four legs in mid-air. If that happens you are now breaking the known laws of physics and something very unusual is taking place!

The Intuitive Pendulum

It's baaaack! I hope you took the time to make your pendulum. We are now going to explore different ways of working with it, keeping with our "mind games" theme. In other words, I will be describing some fun, group exercises.

Make up enough pendulums for you and a group of close friends. Run through the introductory exercises with the pendulum, as detailed in The Intuitive Pendulum chapter of this book. Find someone who had good success with the pendulum. Have that person hold onto it and ask the holder yes or no type questions. For example, have the person concentrate on one of the four suits of playing cards. Then ask, "Are you thinking of hearts?" And so on until you get a yes response. Then verify if that was the actual suit in mind.

You can put a "psychic" twist on this by having someone else think of a suit. You then ask the pendulum operator if the other person is concentrating on hearts, etc. until you get a positive response.

Actually, you can use the pendulum to help you in any of the testing procedures described previously under the heading, It's All in the Cards.

Here's an interesting test. It's one that might demonstrate telepathy or the combined ideomotor actions of two people—you decide!

One person is designated as the sender; the other is the receiver. The receiver holds the pendulum over the "Yes/No" chart found in this book. The sender lightly holds the wrist of the receiver, the wrist of the hand holding the pendulum.

The sender concentrates on either the yes or no response. The pendulum should start to move in one of those two directions. Once a definite swing pattern is apparent, check to see if that was the direction the sender was concentrating on. If you try this test ten times, five correct responses would be chance; six or seven would rate as above average and eight or more would be outstanding!

Many of the exercises already covered in this chapter can be adapted for use with the pendulum. I have already covered how the pendulum can be used in conjunction with the card-testing exercises.

A version of psychometry would be to lay objects on the table and have the pendulum operator hold the pendulum over each object while one of the group stands near the operator or holds onto his or her wrist. The idea here is that the operator tries to locate the object belonging to that specific person by asking (as they hold the pendulum over each object) "Is this _____'s?" using the name of the designated person.

This exercise can be carried out with the objects sealed in envelopes or it can be done with the objects in plain view. You'll get the best results with the objects in plain view and with the designated person holding the operator's wrist.

In the 1920s, pendulums were sold as "sex detectors." You would hold the pendulum over the hand of a pregnant woman. If the pendulum moved in a circle it indicated a female, back and forth movement would represent a male child.

By combining this aspect of pendulum work with the psychometry test just detailed, you can create another exercise.

Have the operator hold the pendulum over each object or envelope. The idea is to use the pendulum to determine if the object belongs to a man or a woman. You can ask, "Does this object belong to a woman?" or you can use the circular motion to represent female and the back and forth motion to signify male.

If you change the procedure to the circular-female, back and forth-male pattern(s), you may want to do a test run first by holding the pendulum over the hands of various people. Note which way the pendulum swings over the hands of men and women to establish your swing pattern. This is basically the same thing you did when you first started to work with the pendulum. In other words, with some operators, the pendulum could respond in a circular pattern for men and a back and forth pattern for women.

Another version of this male/female "sex detector" game is to have each person print his or her name on an index card. The cards are either placed face down on a table or sealed in envelopes and then mixed. The operator holds the pendulum over each card/envelope, getting either a male or female response and the results are checked.

If you want statistical results from any of these male/female tests, you should limit the objects or names to an equal number belonging to men and women. In this way, operators who "hit" on more than 50 percent are scoring above mathematical odds.

Of course, the owner's identities should not be revealed until all the objects/cards have been tested.

The remote viewing test that was covered earlier in this chapter can also be used in conjunction with the pendulum. One of the images would be selected and then the pendulum operator would be asked a series of yes or no questions pertaining to the image: "Is it an outdoor scene?"; "Are people in the photograph?"; etc.

As you know, one application for the pendulum is to ask it personal questions perhaps pertaining to subjects you have been afraid to face. For example, "Am I afraid of having a close relationship? Am I in the right job? Have I chosen the right major? Do I really love so and so?"

A fun adaptation of this application in a group situation would be to have each person hold the pendulum while the group asks the operator personal questions. It's similar to the game Scruples, yet played unconsciously!

I will close this section on the pendulum by describing a dramatic demonstration of pendulum power which may lead to psychokinesis.

Get an empty bottle and suspend the pendulum in the bottle by attaching a needle to the end of the string (opposite the pendulum itself) and inserting the needle into a cork and then corking the bottle.

Place the bottle in the center of a table. Place your hands flat on the table but not touching the bottle. Focus on the bottle and try to get the pendulum to swing within the bottle, hitting the sides. Once you are successful with this, try it with two or more bottles. However, make sure that the strings within the bottles are of different lengths. Focus on a particular bottle and try to get that pendulum alone to move. This can be done as a one-person exercise or you can have a group of people sitting around the table as in the table-tilting demonstration described earlier.

If you have success moving the pendulums within the bottles, you are probably experiencing an advanced form of ideomotor response. However, once you get proficient with this technique, take it one step further. Don't touch the table. Just focus your attention on the pendulums within the bottles. Don't try this until you get really good at causing the pendulums to swing with your hands on the table. I also predict that you will have a greater chance for success with this if you do it with a group of people.

Hairpin Turn

This is a fun, visual exercise in ideomotor response. Get a hairpin and bend the "legs" of it so they are three-quarters of an inch apart. Now, get a ruler. Hold the ruler between your thumb and forefinger at the one-inch end. Hold the ruler parallel to and about one inch from the top of a table. Place the hairpin over the top of the ruler. Concentrate on getting the hairpin to move across the ruler (you may have to give it a push to get it started). See what inch mark you can cause the hairpin to travel to. Don't consciously move the ruler, just focus on the hairpin. You can set up a competition with your friends.

The Mind Motor

This is something I have had a lot of fun with. I've amazed myself with it in private. I've demonstrated it to small groups of people at parties as well as to national television audiences on *Larry King Live,* Lifetime Television and *Crook & Chase.*

It is a simple mind machine. Get a box of matches and a pin or toothpick. Empty all the matches from the box and insert the pin or toothpick into the box. The box is now acting as a kind of stand. The pin or tooth-pick is sticking straight up into the air. Now, get a piece of cardboard about two or three inches square. Fold it diagonally, corner to corner. Unfold it and refold it using the other two corners. Use heavy creases when doing this. Lightly unfold it and pinch in the sides. If you are doing this correctly you will have a small umbrella-looking piece of cardboard. Balance the cardboard on top of the pin/toothpick. Make sure the cardboard "umbrella" can rotate freely and easily atop the pin or toothpick. Cup your hands around the cardboard and focus your attention on it, trying to get it to move with your mind. In a short while, you should see the cardboard begin to rotate. Try to get it to stop and then reverse direction. I guarantee you will have fun with this.

Some people believe it is simply the air currents in a room which cause the cardboard to move. I'm sure that can happen, but I've done the same thing under glass as have a number of other people. See what you think. Try it without any covering at first. Then, as you get proficient with it, seal the motor under something like a Plexiglas pasta container, Tupperware, or the like and cup your hands around the container and try for the same results. It may take quite a bit more time, but I'm betting you can get it to move in this condition as well.

Please don't try it covered until after you've mastered it without the covering. You may only frustrate yourself. Remember, the idea is to have fun!

The Human Lie Detector

Recognizing and reading body language is a fascinating skill. It actually plays a major role in much of my stage work. Let me quickly give you two techniques which will turn you into a human lie detector.

Ask a person to think of a number from one to ten. Now, ask the person to say "no" as you ask, in order, if they are thinking of the number one and so on through ten. Watch their eyes. Right before you name their thought-of number, you will notice that their pupil will dilate. It is most noticeable in gray or blue eyes. Our pupils enlarge when we are stimulated by something.

You can do this same demonstration while feeling the pulse of a person. The pulse should quicken when the person lies.

The Finger Test

Have someone hold out his or her hand, palm down, and ask the person to concentrate on one of his or her four fingers. One at a time, lightly press on the tip of each finger as you say aloud, "Is this the finger?" You will find resistance, the finger will be more rigid, as you touch one of their fingers. This will be the finger the person is concentrating on.

The Eyes Have It

Here's another simple body language stunt you can try on your friends. Take five playing cards and spread them in a fan with the faces of the cards toward your friend. The cards should be evenly spread so that an equal amount of the face of each card is showing. Ask your friend to think of a card. You will notice that your friend's eyes will pause on one particular card. If your friend lets her eyes travel over the face of each card, there will still be a noticeable pause. This is the card your friend is concentrating on.

Now, you just have to reveal the correct card, to your friend's amazement. I suggest that you use a little showmanship. In other words, don't immediately pull the card out of the fan. Close the fan and mix the cards (make sure you remember which card was where as you showed them to your friend). Spread the cards face up toward you and run through them while asking your friend to concentrate on her card. As you look through the cards pull one out, sight unseen to your friend, and place it face down on a table. Ask your friend which card she selected, then ask her to turn the tabled card face up. You should have a match.

As your friend looks at the cards to make her selection, don't be obvious about looking at her eyes. Turn your head away a bit. Your friend should be occupied with looking at the cards and shouldn't notice you watching her eyes.

The interesting thing about these body language stunts is that the more you practice them, the better your ability to read body language becomes. You already process other people's body language on an unconscious level. As you begin to cultivate the habit of processing body language consciously, you will begin to better understand the type of information your unconscious mind has been taking in all along.

Quick, Think of a Number

As important as reading body language is in my work, another important technique I have learned to develop is recognizing the patterns in the way people think. I'll give you a quick example that you can have some fun with.

Get together with a friend and tell the person you are going to try and project a thought into his or her mind. Tell the friend to just relax and say the first thing that pops into his or her mind. You have already recorded your "thought projections" on a piece of paper and have asked the person to hold onto it, without looking at it.

Try this with me now. Quickly,

think of a color,

a wild animal,

a piece of furniture

and a number between one and five.

Given the choices above, most people will choose red, a lion, a chair and the number three. What did you choose?

This chapter was designed to be fun and I hope it succeeded on that level. I also hope that this chapter goes beyond just being fun; I want it to get you to think.

If you played these games, you should have experienced at least a few extraordinary occurrences. Perhaps you experienced things that you wouldn't believe had someone told you that it happened to them.

10 | In Closing

Whatever the mind can conceive
and believe, it can achieve.

Paul H. Dunn

I want to thank you for reading this book. While I attempted to reveal the material in a fun and interactive way, I know that some of you may have had to overcome feelings of uneasiness, doubt or resistance during your reading and experimentation with the exercises in this book. But often that's what it takes when you open up to new worlds of possibilities.

Every great thinker, inventor, innovator or leader has been thought of as a fool at one time. But part of what made them great was their ability to move ahead anyway, trusting their intuition, insight and faith.

I hope that you moved ahead through the chapters of this book. I hope that you experimented with the ideas put forth, worked the exercises and played the games. If so, then you should have experienced the extraordinary and hopefully this caused you to rethink your own definition of what is possible in your life.

I realize that when you delve into the areas explored in this book, you often raise as many questions as you answer. There is always more knowledge to discover. But this shouldn't frustrate you, it should excite you.

The world needs willing explorers, and it is my wish that you will continue to push the envelope, to explore more fully the ideas and concepts I have introduced in this book.

I encourage you to engage those qualities from within, to begin trusting your own intuition, insight and faith and to continue your investigation into the infinite possibilities of the mind.

Have an extraordinary journey!

Notes

Chapter One

1. Time-Life Books, *The Psychics, Mysteries of the Unknown* series (Alexandria, VA: 1992), 109.

2. Daniel Goleman, "Your Unconscious Mind May Be Smarter Than You," *New York Times*, 23 June 1992, sec. C1, p. 11.

Chapter Three

1. Joel Arthur Barker, *Paradigms: The Business of Discovering the Future* (New York: Harper Business, 1993), 73.

2. Time-Life Books, *The Psychics, Mysteries of the Unknown* series (Alexandria, VA: 1992), 109.

3. Roy Rowan, *The Intuitive Manager* (New York: Berkley mass market edition, 1991), 108.

4. Time-Life Books, 108.

5. Rowan, 9.

6. Frances E. Vaughan, *Awakening Intuition* (New York: Anchor Books Doubleday, 1979), 3.

7. Time-Life Books, 109.

8. Rowan, 7-8.

9. Carrie Hedges, "'Hunch' lands a $22m suspect," *USA Today*, 2 September 1997, sec. A., p. 8.

10. Conrad Hilton, *Be My Guest*, (New York: Prentice Hall Press, 1987), 204.

11. Hilton, 204.

12. Willis Harman, Ph.D. and Howard Rheingold, *Higher Creativity*, (New York: Jeremy P. Tarcher/Putnam, 1984), 33.

13. Henry Miller, *Black Spring*, (New York: Grove Press, 1963), 58.

14. Miller, 59.

15. Miller, 59.

16. Ann Oldenburg, "In a word, he's funny," *USA Today*, 25 March 1998, sec. D., p. 2.

17. John Warrack, *Tchaikovsky* (New York: Charles Scribner's Sons, 1973), 131.

18. Warrack, 130.

19. Michael McCall, "Parton returns to the write place," *USA Today*, 25 August 1998, sec. D., p. 1.

20. Marie-Laure Bernadac and Paule DuBouchet, *Picasso—Master of the New Idea*, (New York: Henry N. Abrams, Dec., 1993), 125.

21. Dore Ashton, ed., *Picasso on Art* (New York: Da Capo Press edition, 1972), 9.

Chapter Four

1. Dick Patrick, "The mind holds secrets beyond the zone," *USA Today*, 15 March 1994, sec. C., p. 3.

2. Patrick.

3. Patrick.

4. Patrick.

Bibliography and Suggested Reading

Agor, Weston. *Intuitive Management*. Englewood Cliffs, NJ: Prentice Hall, 1974.

Ashton, Dore, ed. *Picasso On Art*. New York: Da Capo Press, 1972.

Bandler, Richard, and John Grinder. *Frogs Into Princes*. Moab, UT: Real People Press, 1979.

Barker, Joel Arthur. *Paradigms: The Business of Discovering the Future*. New York: Harper Business, 1993.

Bernadac, Marie-Laure, and Paule Du Bouchet. *Picasso—Master of the New Idea*. New York: Harry N. Abrams, Inc., 1993.

Block, Barbara. "Intuition Creeps Out of the Closet and Into the Boardroom." *Management Review,* May 1990, 58-59.

Broughton, Richard. *Parapsychology: The Controversial Science*. New York: Ballantine Books, 1991.

Butt, Dorcas S. *The Psychology of Sport*. New York: Van Nostrand and Reinhold, 1976.

Crichton, Michael. *Travels*. New York: Ballantine Books, 1988.

Crisp, Tony. *Dream Dictionary—A Guide to Dreams and Sleep Experiences*. New York: Dell Publishing, 1990.

Csikszentmihaly, Mihaly. *Flow*. New York: Harper & Row, 1990.

Day, Laura. *Practical Intuition*. New York: Villard Books, 1996.

Dean, Douglas, and John Mihalsky. *Executive ESP*. Englewood Cliffs, NJ: Prentice Hall, 1974.

Delaney, Gayle. *Breakthrough Dreaming*. New York: Bantam Books, 1991.

Freud, Sigmund. *The Interpretation of Dreams*. New York: Avon Books, 1965.

Gittelson, Bernard. *Intangible Evidence*. New York: Simon & Schuster, 1987.

Goldwater, Robert and Marco Treves, ed. *Artists on Art from the XIV to the XX Century*. New York: Pantheon Books, 1972.

Goleman, Daniel. "Your Unconscious Mind May Be Smarter Than You." *The New York Times*, 23 June 1992: C1, 11.

Gris, Henry and William Dick. *The New Soviet Psychic Discoveries*. New York: Warner Books, 1978.

Hilton, Conrad. *Be My Guest*. New York: Prentice Hall, 1987.

Hobson, J. Allan. *The Dreaming Brain*. New York: Basic Books, 1988.

Jackson, Gerald. *Executive ESP*. New York: Pocket Books, 1989.

Jung, C. G. *The Archetypes and the Collective Unconscious*. New York: Princeton/Bollingen, 1990.

_____. ed. *Man and His Symbols*. New York: Anchor Books/ Doubleday, 1964.

Kautz, William. *Intuiting the Future*. New York: Harper & Row, 1989.

Krippner, Stanley, and Joseph Dillard. *Dreamworking*. Buffalo: Bearly Limited, 1988.

Laberge, Stephen. *Lucid Dreaming*. Los Angeles: Jeremy P. Tarcher, 1985.

Lorayne, Harry, and Jerry Lucas. *The Memory Book*. New York: Ballantine Books, 1974.

Meir, Golda. *My Life*. New York: G. P. Putnam & Sons, 1975.

Mintzberg, Henry. "Planning on the Left Side and Managing on the Right." *Harvard Business Review*, July-August 1976, 49-58.

Mishlove, Jeffrey. *Roots of Consciousness*, revised ed. New York: Marlowe and Company, 1993.

Moyers, Bill. *Healing and the Mind*. New York: Doubleday, 1993.

Murphy, Michael, and Rhea White. *In the Zone: Transcendent Experience in Sports*. New York: Penguin/Arkana, 1995.

Naparstek, Belleruth. *Your Sixth Sense*. New York: HarperCollins, 1997.

Nørretranders, Tor. *The User Illusion*. New York: Penguin Books, 1998.

Ostrander, Sheila, and Lynn Schroeder. *Psychic Discoveries Behind the Iron Curtain*. Englewood Cliffs, NJ: Prentice Hall, 1970.

_____. *The ESP Papers: Scientists Speak Out from Behind the Iron Curtain*. New York: Bantam Books, 1976.

Penrose, Roger. *The Emperor's New Mind*. New York: Penguin Books, 1991.

Radin, Dean. *The Conscious Universe—The Scientific Truth of Psychic Phenomenon*. San Francisco: Harper Edge, 1997.

Restak, Richard. *The Brain*. New York: Bantam Books, 1984.

_____. *The Brain, The Last Frontier*. New York: Warner Books, 1979.

_____. *The Mind*. New York: Bantam Books, 1988.

Richardson, Barrie. *The +10% Principle*. San Diego: Pfeiffer & Company, 1993.

Robbins, Anthony. *Unlimited Power*. New York: Ballantine Books, 1986.

Rowan, Roy. *The Intuitive Manager*. New York: Berkley, 1991.

Sanders, Pete. *You Are Psychic*. New York: Macmillan Publishing, 1989.

Schonberg, Harold. *Lives of the Great Composers*. New York: Harper & Row, 1986.

Siegel, Bernie S., M.D. *Love, Medicine & Miracles*. New York: Harper & Row, 1986.

Swan, Ingo. *Natural ESP*. New York: Bantam Books, 1987.

Time-Life Books. *The Psychics, Mysteries of the Unknown* (series). Alexandria, VA: Time-Life Books, 1992.

Vaughan, Frances E. *Awakening Intuition*. New York: Anchor Books/ Doubleday, 1979.

Wolman, Benjamin. *Handbook of Dreams*. New York: Van Nostrand Reinhold, 1979.

Wonder, J. and P. Donovan. *Whole Brain Thinking*. New York: William Morrow, 1984.

Wycoff, Joyce. *Mindmapping*. New York: Berkley Books, 1991.

Index

A

affirmations, 105–14
  conscious/unconscious mind,
    aligning with, 112–13
  creating, 111
  defined, 105–6
  desires, identifying, 108–11
  intuitive pendulum for,
    112–13, 114
  power of, 106–7
  repeating, 113–14
Agor, Weston, on intuition and
  business, 38
alpha brain-waves, 74
artificial intelligence (A.I.), 5–6
association for memory, 22,
  27–29
astral projection, 147–48
automatic writing, 151–53
axons, 3

B

Barker, Joel Arthur, on intuition,
  34

Baxter, Anne, on dreams and
  psychic impressions, 123
bear images in dreams, 127
beta brain-waves, 74
bird images in dreams, 126–27
Blake, William, on dreams and
  scientific insights, 119
blindsight, 136–37
body language games, 181–83
Bohr, Niels, on dreams and scientific insights, 118
Bond, Frederick Bligh, on
  automatic writing, 151
Brahms, Johannes, on dreams
  and creativity, 117
brain as supercomputer, 1–19
  artificial intelligence (A.I.),
    5–6
  axons, 3
  balancing hemispheres, 7
  brainstorming, 8
  capacity of, 1–5
  cocktail party phenomenon,
    15–16

About the Author

Extraordinist Craig Karges is known to millions of television viewers for his entertaining demonstrations of extraordinary phenomena as seen on *The Tonight Show with Jay Leno, Larry King Live, CNN Headline News,* CNBC, E! Entertainment Television, Lifetime Television and The Nashville Network.

Craig's interest in the mysteries of the mind can be traced back to his relationship with his great-uncle (a vaudeville-era stage medium turned spiritualist). At the age of fourteen, Craig began working with his uncle. Upon his uncle's death (one year later), the fifteen-year old Karges inherited his uncle's vast library of books and manuscripts on magic, mentalism, spiritualism, psychology and parapsychology. Delving into his uncle's extensive legacy, Karges discovered many secrets of what is now called extraordinary phenomena. Unfortunately, his great-uncle passed away before completing all of his research. This left the young Karges with many unanswered questions and many mysteries to explore. Craig has spent the last quarter of a century doing just that.

Craig Karges first became popular touring college campuses. He was named "Entertainer of the Year" four times by the National Association for Campus Activities and twice by *Campus Activities Today* magazine. He also was named the most popular variety entertainer on the college circuit for ten consecutive years, as well as being named best male performer and best performing arts attraction.

Even Karges's peers find his work fascinating. He was named the top performer in his field worldwide by the International Psychic Entertainers Association. The National Speakers Association (NSA) honored him with the Certified Speaking Professional (CSP) designation, a recognition bestowed on less than 10 percent of NSA's four thousand-plus members.

Craig Karges says that he does not possess supernatural powers, nor does he claim to perform as a psychic or a magician. While he acknowledges that he is an entertainer, and showmanship plays a role in what he does, he has a standing offer of $100,000, payable to charity, if anyone can prove he uses stooges or confederates in his demonstrations.

Karges currently spends his time traveling the world as both an entertainer and a speaker appearing at theaters, festivals, showrooms, and performing arts centers, as well as universities and corporate events.

As an entertainer, his stage show, "Experience the Extraordinary," is a fantastic blend of mystery, humor, psychology and intuition using total audience participation.

Craig dazzles the mind as he challenges his audiences to question what is real and what is unreal.

He explores the unexplained, the unknown and the unbelievable—all seemingly by the power of the mind. Unspoken thoughts are revealed; predictions are made and verified; matter passes through matter; objects move through the air. As one reviewer put it, "It's like *The Twilight Zone* live on stage. But, it's not frightening; it's fun."

There is a surreal quality to his performance. You will believe it when you see it, but you may not believe what you saw. It is a touch of mystery in a world dominated by technology. And when the curtain falls, you may not be certain whether you were under the spell of an enchanting illusion or have witnessed an extraordinary reality.

As a speaker and workshop presenter, Karges switches his focus from entertainment to empowerment in a highly interactive experience that awakens you to the possibility of reaching your full potential. Participants learn memory techniques; their intuition is tested and they are taught proven techniques of how to tap into their unconscious minds to enhance their creativity, intuition and decision-making processes.

Nothing is impossible in the uncanny world of Craig Karges. No smoke; no mirrors—just today's mysteries that may well become tomorrow's certainties. So get ready to not only *Ignite Your Intuition* but also to "Experience the Extraordinary" with Craig Karges.

To experience Craig Karges live on stage, you can find his tour itinerary on the Web site:

Pollstar magazine: *http://www.pollstar.com*

To contact Craig Karges, please contact his personal management company:

CFB Productions, Inc., P.O. Box 357, Riverton, CT 06065; Telephone: 860-738-3801; Facsimile: 860-738-3805; or email: *cfbprod@aol.com.*

To learn more about Craig Karges, visit his Web site: *http://www.craigkarges.com.*

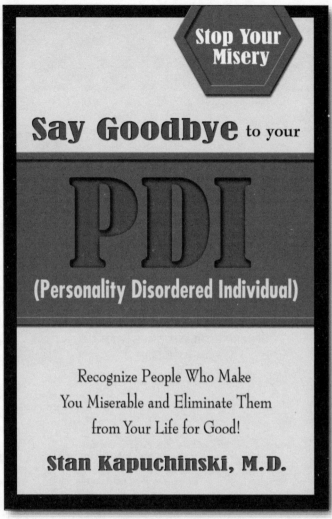

Stop Your Misery

Say Goodbye to your

PDI

(Personality Disordered Individual)

Recognize People Who Make
You Miserable and Eliminate Them
from Your Life for Good!

Stan Kapuchinski, M.D.

Code 6152 • Paperback • $14.95

Eliminate the toxic influence of
personality disordered individuals—whether
they're relatives, friends, or coworkers.

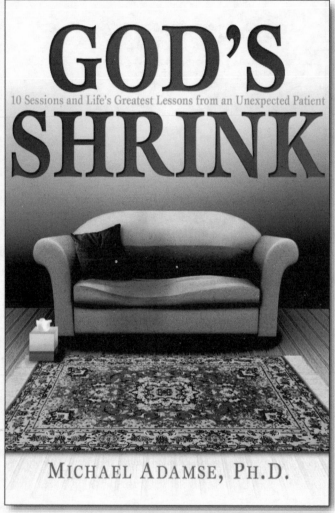